LOUD ENOUGH

Rashid Khan

For my father,
whose quiet strength, unshakable belief in me, and steady presence
lit the path—even when I couldn't see it myself.

CONTENTS

INTRODUCTION

Confidence has become my greatest asset not because I was born with it, but because I learned, sometimes painfully, what happens without it. While intellectual ability is valuable, it's not enough on its own. In today's world, ideas don't rise based on merit alone they rise based on visibility.

Research by Tomas Chamorro-Premuzic (2013) highlights that confidence often outshines competence in real-world settings, and those who speak up even with half-formed ideas are more likely to be seen as leaders. Similarly, Dana Kanze et al. (2017) found that in professional settings, confidence plays a pivotal role in how ideas and individuals are evaluated, often more than their actual substance.

This truth is backed by Amy Cuddy's (2015) research on power posing, which demonstrated how nonverbal expressions of confidence can actually influence how others perceive us and how we perceive ourselves. Albert Bandura's theory of self-efficacy (1997) further explains that belief in our ability to succeed plays a central role in how we think, behave, and feel. Confidence, it turns out, isn't a luxury it's a performance amplifier.

I learned this firsthand. In high school, I was the classic overthinker obsessing over every detail, rehearsing endlessly, and chasing a perfect version of everything I did. While I earned high marks, I constantly second-guessed my worth. Meanwhile, a classmate with less preparation but more presence would breeze through presentations, crack jokes, and still capture attention and praise. It frustrated me. Not because he didn't deserve to be heard but because I did too, and I wasn't giving myself permission.

Angela Duckworth's research on grit (2016) also affirmed that perseverance, not perfectionism, drives long-term achievement. This book is about learning to take that step — about developing confidence not as a trait you either have or don't, but as a skill you train.

Hello,

I have been contemplating the factors that contribute to confidence, and I have discovered that it is a skill that can be developed through self-belief. Contrary to popular belief, confidence is not an innate trait; rather, it is a construct that can be cultivated.

It is important to recognise that perfection is not a prerequisite for confidence. Rather, it is the willingness to take action even when one feels uncertain that truly matters. This proactive approach is the key to building confidence.

I personally do not wait for confidence to manifest; instead, I simply begin to move forward, and confidence naturally follows suit. This principle forms the foundation of my book. It is not about adopting a false persona or pretending to possess complete knowledge. Instead, it is about learning to overcome fear, doubt, and the internal voice that questions one's abilities.

If you aspire to transform your life, the first step is to alter this internal dialogue. By ceasing to wait for a state of readiness, you can take decisive action. Even if you encounter setbacks, you will eventually learn from them. Confidence is not a magical ability; it is a result of consistent effort and perseverance.

I am here to assist you in developing your confidence. It is important to acknowledge that you are not seeking to lack talent; rather, you are motivated by the desire to observe others with lesser abilities achieving success. Individuals who speak up, take risks, and garner attention, even when they lack comprehensive knowledge, serve as inspiration. Meanwhile, you possess ideas, potential, and drive, yet you remain hesitant to pursue your aspirations.

You may be waiting for the opportune moment, the ideal time, or the manifestation of confidence. However, I must inform you that this moment will not arrive. The most significant revelation is that you are capable of more than you currently perceive. Despite encountering obstacles, you persist in your pursuit.

One crucial aspect that is often overlooked is the significance of confidence in relation to talent. Without confidence, talent remains largely untapped.

Zero.
Nada.

In the world, success is not solely attributed to intelligence or experience. It is bestowed upon those who demonstrate courage and willingness to contribute. Even when their voices tremble, they dare to speak up and raise their hands. While this may sound harsh, it is essential to recognise that your purpose here is not to indulge in superficiality, but to awaken and break free from the limitations that hold you back.

The key to unlocking confidence, which is not a mere personality trait but a skill that can be acquired, is to grasp this fundamental principle. Allow me to illustrate my understanding through a personal anecdote. If you have ever felt like an outsider, observing others take action while you remain on the sidelines, you will find resonance in this story.

Not here for fluff—you're here to wake up. And the fastest way to snap out of whatever has been holding you back is to understand this one thing: Confidence is not a personality trait. It's a skill. And it's one you can learn. Let me show you how I know. Because if you've ever felt like you're on the sidelines while everyone else is out there taking the shots, you're going to see yourself in this story.

Meet Jessica: smart, thoughtful, and great at her job. She's the kind of person everyone relies on, but no one really notices. Always working behind the scenes, quietly making sure things don't fall apart, Jessica's coworkers love her, and her manager praises her dependability. She has the performance reviews, qualifications, and brainpower. What she doesn't have is a seat at the table, a voice in the room, or the guts to raise her hand when it counts.

You know what that feels like, don't you? Sitting in a meeting with an idea that could change everything, but staying silent. Watching other people take credit for half-baked ideas while you're still perfecting yours. Smiling politely while your gut screams, "I should've said something." Jessica had that moment more times than she could count. She told herself it wasn't fear—it was strategy. She was being smart, patient, and careful. But deep down, she knew the truth: she was scared. Scared of sounding stupid, scared of being wrong, and scared of being seen.

She kept telling herself she needed more confidence, that one day, it would just… show up.

Spoiler: It didn't.

Enter Rachel: Now Rachel? She is the opposite. Bold, loud, and quick to speak, even quicker to act. She does not overthink or apologise. She throws out ideas like darts some hit, some do not but she never hesitates. She owns her space as if she was born to take it. Jessica watched her in awe, and sometimes, let's be honest, with a little resentment, because Rachel did not always have better ideas. She was not always right. But she was seen, she was in the spotlight, and more often than not, she got what Jessica wanted: the attention, the praise, the opportunities.

Jessica could not understand it. How does she do it? she would wonder. Is she just wired differently? Was she born confident?

No.

Rachel lacked confidence in her abilities. However, she discovered a crucial insight before Jessica did: perfection is not always rewarded; rather, action is valued.

A pivotal moment occurred during a routine Thursday meeting. The team was grappling with a project, and despite the lack of enthusiasm, everyone feigned interest. Jessica, with remarkable foresight, identified the crux of the matter and the potential solution. Her understanding was profound, and she began to articulate her findings. However, a moment of hesitation overcame her, and she paused, contemplating the possibility of being incorrect or being met with resistance.

At that critical juncture, Rachel proposed an idea that lacked the essential components. Nevertheless, she presented it with such conviction that the room was captivated, drawing their attention and prompting them to lean in for more. Consequently, they engaged in a brainstorming session. Jessica sat there, visibly astonished, not because Rachel had spoken, but because she had remained silent. That moment shattered something within her. She realised that she was not lacking in talent; rather, she was lacking the courage to express herself. Consequently, she made a transformative change. She took a courageous step by raising her hand, her voice slightly trembling, and her palms perspiring. However, she presented the actual solution, guiding them through it with clarity, logic, and solidity. The room fell silent, and her supervisor inquired, "Why haven't we heard more from you before?"

That marked the initial domino effect. Jessica's transformation did not transpire abruptly, but a subtle shift emerged, a fissure in the barrier she had erected around her voice.

The most striking aspect is that she was unaware of having employed a potent instrument. It was a fleeting yet potent action underpinned by scientific principles and human behaviour. This technique modifies the brain's chemical composition and enables individuals to transcend their fears. Although she had never been explicitly instructed in its use, she instinctively sensed its potency, yet had never identified it.

However, I have identified it. It is straightforward, scientifically proven, and effective.

This is the same tool I have employed to overcome depression and find the strength to rise from bed, to speak on stages despite feeling like an imposter, to transition careers, launch innovative ideas, and engage in challenging conversations. It is the very tool you will learn about in this book.

But not yet.

For now, it is essential to comprehend that confidence is not an emotion; it is a conscious decision. It is time to make yours. Allow me to share a silent truth that everyone acknowledges: confidence is the decisive factor in determining who is heard, seen, and selected.

Not talent, not intelligence, nor the quality of one's ideas are the determining factors.

The world does not await perfection; it anticipates your presence. Individuals who garner recognition, advancement, remembrance, and respect are not always the most exceptional. They are the ones who possess the audacity to raise their hands, express their opinions, and seize opportunities. Confidence is the catalyst that propels you into the room, sustains your presence at the table, and compels others to acknowledge your worth.

Many individuals experience a sense of stagnation, opting for safety, maintaining a submissive demeanour, and patiently awaiting their turn. However, this strategy may not yield the desired results. You may find yourself weary of witnessing others seize chances that you were too apprehensive to pursue. You may yearn to articulate your desires yet remain silent. You may perform at only 90% of your potential due to the fear of revealing your true self.

It is crucial to recognise that you are not broken, indolent, or weak. You undermine your own potential daily by harbouring the misconception that confidence is a privilege reserved for others.

This notion must cease.

This book is not about faking it until you make it. It is not about pretending to be someone you are not. It is not about yelling affirmations in the mirror or trying to become the loudest person in the room. This is about learning the real truth no one told you: Confidence is a skill. And it is learnable. By the end of this book, here's what's going to change:

1. You will cease waiting to feel prepared. Please reread that statement. The most prevalent misconception that has hindered your progress is this: I will express myself when I feel more confident. Contrary to popular belief, you will never truly feel ready. Confidence precedes action; it emerges from action. You will acquire the ability to act before doubt ensnares you.

2. You will silence the internal critic that has been controlling your life. You are familiar with the voice I am referring to—the one that exclaims, "Who do you believe you are?" That voice is not an authentic representation of you; it is merely fear. It has been the driving force behind your decisions. You will learn how to interrupt, silence, and reprogram it so that it ceases to hinder your progress.

3. You will cultivate the confidence habit that can be executed in mere seconds. Jessica, I, and countless others have successfully employed it. This approach is scientifically validated and behaviourally proven. Once you master it, you will possess the

ability to summon confidence at any moment—before a meeting, a conversation, or even when sending that daunting email.

4. You will establish unshakable self-trust. Confidence is not synonymous with perpetual correctness; it encompasses the assurance that you will endure even when you are mistaken. It is the grounded certainty that empowers you to take risks, speak freely, and break free from the silence of conformity.

5. You will commence living your life assertively. Loudly, boldly, and authentically. No longer will you play small, shrink to fit, or await permission. You will articulate your thoughts and feelings unequivocally. You will cease self-doubt and second-guessing every action. Most importantly, you will cease sacrificing your well-being for the comfort of others.

Allow me to clarify: this transformation does not occur overnight. It is not a magical solution. However, it is a genuine process. Each chapter in this book represents a step forward, a gentle push to emerge from your comfort zone and reclaim your power. You do not need to transform into someone else to feel confident; you merely need to reconnect with your true self. And that, my friend, is precisely what we are accomplishing here.

One small, courageous, and transformative decision at a time.

PART 1

UNDERSTANDING OF THE PROBLEMS

How to Break Free from the Lie Keeping You Small

"I'll do it when I feel ready" is a myth

For decades, researchers have revealed a silent epidemic that keeps capable people playing small. In 1978, psychologists Pauline Clance and Suzanne Imes first identified the Phenomenon—where high-achievers internalize self-doubt and downplay success, fearing they'll be exposed as "frauds." Since then, studies across cultures, from Indian college students to global professionals, show over 60% of people experience this at some point. The real culprit? Fear, perfectionism, and a mindset conditioned to equate readiness with worthiness.

As psychologist Carol Dweck's research proves, the fixed mindset traps us into believing our abilities are static—and that we must wait until we're "perfect" to act

---

Let us confront the reality: we will never truly feel prepared to take action. Whether it is speaking up in a meeting, increasing your rates, initiating the business, taking the stage, or publishing a daunting post, the longer you delay the manifestation of confidence, the longer you will remain stagnant. We engage in a comforting illusion, convincing ourselves that we will act when we feel ready. However, let us acknowledge that readiness is a delusion your mind employs to maintain comfort.

Consider this: has "ready" ever truly manifested?

Have you felt prepared to leave a toxic relationship? Did you feel ready the first time you ventured into something novel? Did you feel utterly prepared the moment before sending a significant request or raising your hand in a room filled with intimidating individuals?

Clearly not. For readiness is not an emotion; it is a decision.

The True Reason for Procrastination Allow me to share a profound revelation I have gained through personal experience. When you utter, "I will do it when I am ready," what you truly convey is…

"Fear." Fear of making a mistake, of appearing foolish, of disappointing others, and of failure.

Consequently, you postpone your action. You seek additional information, hoping for the perfect moment. What appears to be preparation is merely procrastination cloaked in a well-fitted outfit.

Consider this pivotal moment: The Phone Call That Altered My Path. A few years ago, I found myself lying on the edge of my bed, holding my phone in my hand, fixated on the number of a senior executive with whom I had previously held a meeting—eight months prior. I possessed an idea, a show concept that I held dear. Nevertheless, the prospect of actually calling her sent shivers down my spine. My stomach churned, and I felt my fear exerting its usual influence, attempting to dissuade me.

"What if she perceives my incompetence?"
"She likely has forgotten about you."
"You are not adequately prepared for this endeavour."

In that moment, I realised something profound that would alter my approach: if I continued to wait for a state of confidence, I would never take decisive action.

Therefore, I set a timer and proceeded with the call. While I lacked confidence, I felt a sense of pride. I had not relied on courage; instead, I had generated it.

The Science Behind the Myth: Contrary to popular belief, confidence does not precede action; rather, it emerges after it. When we confront a challenging task, our brains perceive it as a success. Each small victory contributes to the growth of self-assurance. Our minds begin to acknowledge our ability to handle the situation. Conversely, hesitation triggers a perception of danger. We train ourselves to freeze, retreat, and postpone action indefinitely.

Unfortunately, the concept of "someday" never materialises.

The confident version of yourself is not an abstract concept; she is already present, albeit unspoken. You have simply not permitted her to express herself yet.

Remember Jessica?

She did not raise her hand because she felt courageous; rather, she did so because a small, determined part of her was ready to break free from the limitations imposed upon her. She had exhausted the waiting game for confidence to manifest in a pre-determined form. She acted before the doubt could gain the upper hand. This book is about embracing the absence of readiness, dispensing with pretence, and taking action regardless.

This chapter serves as a wake-up call. Your dream, your desired change, your envisioned version of yourself—she is already in motion, patiently awaiting your action.

Take the initiative and embrace the reality.

Fear is a master of disguise. It does not manifest solely as a racing heart or sweaty palms. Occasionally, it assumes the guise of a sharp suit, carrying a clipboard labeled "Logic," "Planning," or "Preparation." Its convincing nature often leads us to believe we are being manipulated.

You may find yourself rationalising:
"I must conduct further research before commencing."
"The opportune moment has not arrived."
"Patience is the virtue; I should wait until all aspects are clarified."

These rationalisations are not strategies; they are stall tactics. Fear masquerades as a clever disguise, whispering sweet nothings to maintain your current state.

The Illusion of Safety

Brain seeks certainty, yearning to safeguard from failure, embarrassment, and rejection. Consequently, it convinces that remaining in the planning phase is prudent, that gathering more information is wise, and that waiting until feel "ready" is responsible. However, the truth is, it is not safeguarding; it is paralysing and mistake inaction for intelligence, allowing fear to dictate actions.

The Planning Trap

Consider a friend of mine, Rachel. She had a brilliant business idea. She dedicated months to crafting the ideal business plan, meticulously researching every detail, attending workshops, and meticulously refining her website. Despite her efforts, she never launched her business.

The reason behind her hesitation remains unclear.

The Perils of Over-Preparation

Planning is undoubtedly important, but there exists a delicate balance between thorough preparation and paralysis. When you find yourself perpetually engaged in endless planning, it is crucial to introspect and ask yourself: are you gathering information to progress or avoiding action?

Is this planning generating momentum or creating a comfortable sanctuary? Remember, action is the antidote to fear, not more planning or research.

Remember, confidence does not emanate from possessing complete knowledge; it arises from taking tangible action. Therefore, resist the allure of fear masquerading as logic. Recognise its true nature and proceed with the next step, no matter how insignificant it may seem. The life you aspire to is not achieved through flawless plans; it is realised through bold actions.

While confidence may not precede action, it can be cultivated through consistent effort. Therefore, prioritise action over the pursuit of confidence.

I frequently encounter individuals expressing their desire to initiate a new venture but expressing a lack of confidence. They anticipate gaining confidence before taking action, such as speaking up in meetings, requesting a raise, or applying for a job.

However, the truth is that such confidence does not spontaneously arise; it is cultivated through consistent effort and action. Becoming confident does not involve merely contemplating speaking up; it arises from actually taking the plunge and experiencing the subsequent realisation of survival. Similarly, endless resume tweaking does not lead to confidence; it stems from applying, interviewing, making mistakes, and learning from them.

Therefore, confidence is not the initial spark; it is the subsequent smoke that emerges from consistent action.

Have you ever ignited a fire? There is no smoke without a flame. Similarly, confidence requires action. It is the risk, the step, and the daunting task that instills fear. Confidence manifests as the smoke that emerges afterward. The adrenaline rush experienced when taking a courageous action is not fear; it is your body preparing to establish a new level of self-assurance.

It communicates, “You have accomplished something. You have survived. You can repeat this process.” Each iteration of this process reinforces trust. Self-belief is not acquired through thinking; it is achieved through action.

Let us revisit Jessica’s story.

The individual who finally raised her hand during the high-stakes strategy meeting? Do you believe she felt confident when she did so? Absolutely not. She felt her voice tremble, her hands perspire, and she feared uttering an unwise remark. Nevertheless, she took action. And that moment, that vulnerable and shaky moment, did not merely alter how others perceived her; it profoundly transformed her self-perception. It rewired her brain, demonstrating to her, "I possess the ability to handle challenging tasks."

The power of acting before feeling prepared lies in this very fact. You are not lacking confidence; you are lacking evidence. Evidence that you can speak up without succumbing to anxiety, that you can initiate something and navigate the learning curve, that you can take risks without crumbling under pressure.

How do you obtain such evidence? By engaging in the action itself. Even if you are apprehensive, shaky, or even with your heart pounding in chest. For one bold move can transform everything. Not because it renders fearless, but because it affirms strength to overcome fear.

That is confidence.

It may not be ostentatious or always aesthetically pleasing, but it becomes the moment cease waiting and commence acting.

Confidence does not await you passively; rather, it conceals itself behind the next action you are apprehensive about undertaking. I assure you that once you take that initial step, confidence will swiftly manifest. By employing the logic provided in this book, you can discern its true nature and then take the next step, no matter how small. Remember that the life you desire is not found in perfect plans; it is found in bold actions.

Summary: The notion that confidence precedes action is a misconception. Confidence is cultivated through proactive actions, not passive anticipation. Fear frequently masquerades as rationality, resulting in procrastination and inaction.

How to Silence the Voice That Doubts You

Research shows that up to 80% of our daily thoughts are negative, and much of that self-talk is automatic and critical (Boer, 2023). Psychologists Pauline Clance and Suzanne Imes (1978) first described this pattern in high-achievers, calling it the "Impostor Phenomenon." Since then, studies have shown that chronic negative self-talk fuels anxiety, low self-worth, and self-sabotage.

Lena possessed a demeanour that suggested a constant sense of self-consciousness. In professional settings, she maintained a reserved approach, concealing her thoughts internally, akin to handwritten notes that she refrained from sharing aloud. During social gatherings, her laughter was often delayed, accompanied by a pervasive gaze that seemed to seek validation from others.

While she may not have exhibited overt shyness, a persistent internal dialogue served as a formidable obstacle. This internal voice, akin to a silent critic, instilled in her a pervasive sense of inadequacy, urging her to be cautious, as she lacked sufficient knowledge and feared the potential for embarrassment.

Despite the invisible presence of this voice, it resonated profoundly with Lena, akin to a deafening echo.

One Thursday afternoon, Lena was entrusted with presenting a small project she had diligently led to success. The presentation consisted of a ten-minute update, devoid of groundbreaking content. However, as she stood in the hallway outside the meeting room, her heart experienced a palpable surge of anxiety.

She observed her reflection in the glass window—a professional, composed, and polished individual yet the internal voice persisted, offering disparaging remarks such as "You're not good at this" and "They'll see through you." Additionally, she was plagued by the question, "Why can't you be like her?" (Although the identity of "her" remained elusive, Lena often envisioned someone taller, more assertive, and more accomplished.)

Let us clarify that the internal voice she experiences is a deceiver. It engages in self-doubt, presents pessimistic scenarios, and replays past errors incessantly, akin to a repetitive Netflix series you never sought. The most concerning aspect is your acceptance of this voice. Daily, you allow it to make decisions on your behalf. You retreat from opportunities, second-guess your intuition, and remain silent when your inner voice urges expression. The reason behind this behaviour is your erroneous belief that the internal voice constitutes truth.

However, it is not.

It is merely a malfunction in your cognitive process. Today, we embark on a journey to rectify this malfunction.

Confronting Your Inner Critic: The Persistent Inner Critic

Imagine this scenario:

Within your mind, you reside with a toxic roommate who relentlessly critiques every aspect of your life—your attire, your speech, your decisions, your physical appearance, and even your aspirations. In the real world, you would not tolerate such behaviour from a physical individual. Yet, within the confines of your mind, this individual holds dominion.

This inner critic manifests in various forms, such as:

Self-doubt: "Who do you think you are?"
Fear of failure: "You're going to mess this up."
Ageism: "You're too old for this."
Inadequacy: "You're not ready."
Public ridicule: "They're going to laugh at you."

These negative thoughts can be quite familiar. The truth is, you have been seeking life advice from someone who lacks the expertise to guide you effectively. It is time to recognise and address this persistent inner critic.

The Genesis of the Inner Critic

The inner critic did not originate from you; rather, it was formed over time through the accumulation of negative experiences. Through the piecemeal accumulation of negative feedback, such as comments from others, errors made, and past embarrassments, your brain developed a pattern of self-doubt. In an attempt to safeguard itself from potential emotional distress, brain created a narrator a voice that maintains a state of caution, silence, and perceived safety.

However, it is pertinent to consider the following question:

From what does this safety stem?

Rejection? Failure? Judgment?

Let me tell you something about those three things:
Rejection won't kill you. Failure is the catalyst for learning. Judgment is never personal; it is always directed at others. Despite this understanding, you allow that internal voice to hinder your life's progress.

The Thought Does Not Equate to Truth

Merely believing something does not make it factual. For those who may not have fully grasped this concept, it is crucial to remember that: brain functions as a survival mechanism, primed to detect potential threats rather than constructing an ideal life. As a result, it tends to adopt a negative outlook, engages in excessive overthinking, and resorts to defensive strategies. The voice in your mind is not a reliable source of intuition or a manifestation of your higher self; it is merely a manifestation of noise.

Allow me to provide you with an account of Rachel's journey.

Rachel was experiencing a state of stagnation. She possessed a wealth of ideas, yet she consistently failed to translate them into tangible action. Whenever she was on the verge of commencing her side hustle, a persistent internal voice would emerge, assailing her with doubts such as:

- "You lack the necessary qualifications."
- "Your knowledge is insufficient."
- "The venture is destined for failure."

Consequently, Rachel would revert to the planning and tinkering phase, patiently awaiting the opportune moment when the internal voice would proclaim, "This is the opportune time." However, it is important to note that this elusive moment never materialised.

Scientific Explanation

Your brain is programmed to prioritise survival over self-assurance. When confronted with uncertainty or unfamiliar situations, your amygdala initiates a fight-or-flight response. It transmits signals such as "Danger!" "Retreat!" and "Stay small!"

However, it is imperative to acknowledge that you are not defined by your amygdala's responses. You are not your fear. You are not your doubts. You are not the critical voice in your mind. You are the individual perceiving the voice. Consequently, you possess the ability to engage in dialogue. Literally, engage in verbal communication with it.

The Origins of Self-Doubt

Your inner critic did not emerge spontaneously. It was constructed over time. Perhaps it originated from a teacher who humiliated you during public speaking, a parent who consistently criticised your shortcomings, or a moment of failure that led your brain to conclude, "Never risk such a setback again." Gradually, these experiences became narratives, and these narratives became your inner dialogue. You have been traversing life listening to an outdated record that asserts your inadequacy in intelligence, capability, attractiveness, and worthiness.

This assertion is unsubstantiated. However, unless you encounter evidence to the contrary, you will continue to believe it as fact.

The True Cost of the Inner Critic

The inner critic can have a detrimental impact on your life. Consider the following consequences:

Missed Opportunities: You may miss out on potential opportunities due to self-doubt and fear of failure.
Damaged Relationships: The inner critic can sabotage relationships before they have even begun.
Diminished Dreams: You may downgrade your dreams into mere hobbies.
Unapplied Opportunities: You may overlook job opportunities that align with your skills and interests.
Unlaunched Ideas: You may suppress innovative ideas that could have a significant impact.
Missed Chance to Change: You may remain silent when your voice could have made a positive difference.

The inner critic is not merely concerned with self-confidence; it encompasses your entire life. By permitting it to dictate your actions, you restrict your potential and hinder your development into the most fulfilling version of yourself.

By now, you have likely recognised that the internal voice that criticises you, deems you inadequate, and hinders your progress has been exerting undue influence for an extended period. However, have you ever paused to contemplate the rationale behind your belief in this voice?

Why, when it advises against speaking up, does your body react as if it has encountered a supernatural presence? Why, when it asserts your lack of qualifications, do you retreat and shrink as if it were an absolute truth? The answer lies in the fact that your brain has been conditioned to accept these beliefs. Indeed, it is not a reflection of your inherent flaws, weaknesses, or lack of confidence. Rather, it is a consequence of your brain operating a program, a habitual cycle that has been perpetuated for years.

Allow me to elucidate.

Brain's Primary Function is Not Happiness, brain's primary concern is not happiness. What truly matters to brain is survival. Brain is not designed to thrive, reach goals, or live a dream life. Its sole purpose is to ensure your continued existence. This biological predisposition has persisted for thousands of years. The voice of self-doubt is a protective mechanism employed by brain to safeguard from potential pain, rejection, failure, embarrassment, and any perceived "threat."

However, there is a fundamental issue:

Brain lacks the distinction between life-threatening situations, such as being pursued by a tiger, and seemingly insignificant tasks like sending a risky email, delivering a presentation, going live on Instagram, or expressing true feelings to others. It simply perceives "uncertainty" and triggers a defensive response, akin to an "abort mission." This is why you freeze, procrastinate, and shrink yourself.

It is not fear. It is a wiring. And the more you obey it, the stronger it becomes.

The Habit Loop

The crux of the matter lies in the transformation of thoughts into habits.

Consider this scenario: whenever you contemplate speaking in a meeting, an internal voice emerges, assuring you of your inadequacy in comparison to others. This belief leads to silence, self-disappointment, and the perpetuation of a cycle.

Trigger: The thought of speaking up.
Thought: "Avoid uttering foolishness."
Action: Refrain from speaking.
Reward: Escape discomfort.

Your brain recognises and associates this pattern with "Safety = Goodness." Consequently, it repeats the same sequence in subsequent encounters. The frequency of this cycle deepens the neural pathway, resulting in the thought becoming an automatic response rather than a conscious decision. As a consequence, you no longer merely perceive a lack of confidence; you genuinely believe it.

This belief has been reinforced by the development of an identity centred around it. Brain has made it familiar, and the repeated cycle has imbued it with a sense of truth.

You Are Not the Problem; the Pattern Is.

Let us clarify this unequivocally:

You are not "lacking in confidence." You have simply developed a habit of self-doubt. Unconsciously, you have trained your brain to second-guess, overanalyze, and remain submissive. However, if you have conditioned your brain into this cycle, you can extricate it.

Neuroscience 101: Unraveling the Mysteries of the Mind

Let us delve into the fascinating world of the brain, exploring its intricate workings without becoming overly technical. Each thought you generate triggers a specific set of neurons within brain. The frequency with which you engage in a particular thought strengthens the neural connection, akin to a trail in a forest that becomes more worn down with each iteration of use. Over time, this trail transforms into the path of least resistance. This phenomenon explains how negative thought patterns manifest in our minds. Brain naturally responds with, "You can't do this," more readily than with, "You've got this." This is because negative thought patterns are easier, more familiar, and more efficient. However, efficiency does not equate to helpfulness.

If you aspire to forge a new trail, it is essential to challenge conventional thinking and embrace alternative perspectives. You've got to walk a different path. Again and again. On purpose. That's how you build new wiring. It's called neuroplasticity. Brain can rewire itself at any age. But it only rewires through action not intention.

You can read all the confidence books you desire, watch all the TED talks, and journal your fears into oblivion. However, until you take a new action while the old fear persists you are not breaking the cycle.

Overcoming Fear: The Importance of Action

It is a common misconception that one can simply think their way into courage. In reality, if you could logically reason your way into confidence, you would have already achieved it. You possess intelligence, have read relevant literature, and have meticulously replayed scenarios in your mind, attempting to overcome fear through rational thought.

However, the reality is that this approach often leads to increased anxiety, procrastination, and perfectionism, ultimately resulting in inaction. The crucial truth that many individuals resist acknowledging is that fear cannot be overcome through mere thought. Instead, it must be confronted and managed through action. This is the point where most individuals encounter difficulty. They anticipate the fear's eventual disappearance, expressing sentiments such as:

- "Once I feel prepared…"
- "Once I am more confident…"
- "Once I have fully comprehended the situation…"

No, that is not preparation.
It is fear disguised as yoga pants, sipping a latte, and calling itself "preparation." It is a trap, and it is very effective at sounding responsible. However, it is not. It is resistance, hesitation, and fear attempting to hinder your potential.

Fear's Purpose: Safeguarding, Not Achievement

It is crucial to understand that fear is not inherently malevolent; rather, it serves as a protective mechanism for our survival. When our brain perceives potential risks, fear intervenes to prevent us from experiencing embarrassment, rejection, or failure.

However, it is essential to recognise that fear lacks the distinction between "danger" and "discomfort." It responds uniformly regardless of the nature of the perceived threat, whether it is stepping onto a TED stage or entering oncoming traffic. This physiological response, characterised by rapid heart rate, dry mouth, and heightened brain activity, signals the body's natural fight-or-flight response.

Allowing fear to serve as a sole deterrent can lead to a state of stagnation and prevent individuals from achieving their goals. The key to overcoming fear lies in taking decisive action, regardless of the perceived challenges. By doing so, individuals can break free from the cycle of fear and progress towards their objectives.

How to Move Forward When You're Too Smart to Fail

Being intelligent doesn't always mean you'll move faster — sometimes, it means you'll stall longer. Research by Carol Dweck (2006), Angela Duckworth (2016), and Adam Grant (2021) highlights a striking paradox: those with high intelligence often fear failure more than others, because their identity is tied to being "smart." This creates what psychologists call a "fixed mindset trap," where instead of taking bold steps forward, we stay stuck in analysis, perfectionism, or self-doubt. The smarter we are, the better we become at justifying inaction. This chapter unpacks the hidden weight of intelligence — and how to finally use your gifts not as anchors, but as wings.

Being smart can sometimes work against you. Studies show that high intelligence often correlates with overthinking, perfectionism, and a fear of failure—traits that lead to analysis paralysis and avoidance (Dweck, 2006; Nolen-Hoeksema, 2000). Dr. Carol Dweck's groundbreaking research on mindset theory revealed that people with a fixed mindset tend to believe their abilities are static, making them more likely to avoid risks where they might not excel. In contrast, a growth mindset embraces learning through failure. Similarly, Bandura's theory of self-efficacy (1977) emphasizes that belief in your ability to succeed grows not through thought, but through action. The more you act—even imperfectly—the more capable you feel. Neuroscientist Barbara Oakley (2014) also found that intellectual overanalyzers often struggle with forward momentum because their brains favor reflection over execution. The truth is, thinking smarter doesn't always lead to doing better. Moving forward means trusting action more than answers.

Let us be candid for a moment. You are not indolent, unmotivated, or incapable. You possess intelligence and the ability to achieve your goals. Why, then, are you still experiencing stagnation? Why do you persist in holding onto ideas that resonate with you? Why do you engage in self-sabotage by talking yourself out of taking action, raising your hand, seeking opportunities, and demonstrating your readiness in the manner that aligns with your potential?

It is not because you lack the necessary qualifications. It is because mind is working against you in the most sophisticated and persuasive manner imaginable. Intelligent individuals encounter obstacles not because they lack the necessary preparation, but because they have trained their minds to engage in excessive overanalysis, overpreparation, and self-doubt, leading to a state of paralysis. If this resonates with you, then it is a positive sign. Once you comprehend the intricacies of this trap, you can effectively break free from it.

Allow me to illustrate this process for you.

The Intelligence Trap: When Thinking Becomes Concealment

Intelligent individuals, particularly those who excel, possess a remarkable ability to anticipate potential challenges. They engage in continuous mental simulations, contemplating scenarios such as mistakes, judgments, inadequacy, and imperfections. However, this analytical prowess, which facilitates effective problem-solving in professional settings, can become a hindrance when applied to personal endeavours. Instead of preparing proactively, individuals may resort to procrastination, albeit disguised as rationalisation.

The perception of intelligence often leads to the belief that waiting for the ideal moment is the optimal approach. However, this mindset can be mistaken for procrastination. In reality, individuals may be stalling, seeking perfection, rationalising their actions, and avoiding responsibility. The underlying reason for this behaviour lies in the inherent nature of fear. While fear may manifest in overt forms, such as screaming toddlers, it often presents itself in more subtle and sophisticated ways. For instance, it may manifest as a business suit-clad individual carrying a clipboard, offering suggestions like:

- “Let’s wait until we are 100% certain.”
- “It would be prudent to take another course first.”
- “Perhaps we should double-check the plan once more.”

These rationalisations, while appearing reasonable, are merely disguises for fear. The longer individuals succumb to these rationalisations, the more entrenched they become in their current state.

Intelligent Individuals Require Approval to Embrace Imperfection Initially

Contrary to popular belief, the more intellectually gifted an individual becomes, the more challenging it becomes to relinquish a beginner’s mindset. Accustomed to competence, capability, and respect, the concept of embarking on a journey where potential inadequacy, even temporarily, may arise can be daunting. The allure of remaining on the sidelines, diligently refining ideas, outweighs the risk of being perceived as attempting and failing.

However, confidence is not solely acquired in private settings or through extensive research; it is cultivated through action. It is imperative to grant oneself permission to acknowledge initial imperfections. To stumble over words, share an awkward video, or express consent before fully prepared.

It is through these actions that individuals admired achieve their accomplishments. Their success is not attributed to fearlessness, but rather to their willingness to confront and overcome it.

The Hidden Burden of Overthinking

You may perceive yourself as being cautious and strategic. However, let us be candid: Overthinking manifests as fear in comfortable attire. It appears to be self-awareness, but it is merely a repetitive cycle of self-doubt. Not only does it hinder your progress; it also drains your energy. The constant mental agitation leads to exhaustion and frustration with your own inaction.

The sense of imposterhood arises not from a lack of authenticity, but rather from the absence of evidence that contradicts your self-perception. If you seek clarity, confidence, and momentum, cease waiting for a state of readiness. Refrain from thinking your way out of challenges and commence taking action. Even if it involves small steps or imperfect progress, take the first step forward.

Action: The Ultimate Filter for Personal Growth

While planning is undoubtedly valuable, it is not the sole determinant of success. True certainty is achieved through action. Each small step taken generates valuable data, and every courageous endeavour, even if imperfect, provides proof of progress and resilience. The distinction between individuals who realise their potential and those who do not lies in their mindset. The former ceases to dwell on thoughts and embraces action.

This fundamental shift is not attributed to superior intellect, ample time, or absence of fear. Rather, it stems from the simple act of movement.

Challenging the Myth of Readiness: A Comprehensive Examination

Contrary to popular belief, there is no such thing as absolute readiness for any endeavour, including public speaking, taking risks, or embracing change. Confidence is not a prerequisite; rather, it is a consequence of taking action. The longer individuals procrastinate, the more entrenched they become in their comfort zones. Intelligent individuals tend to delay, while courageous individuals seize opportunities and move forward.

These latter-day adventurers prioritise action over perfection, sacrificing the pursuit of ideal outcomes for immediate progress.

Fear's Silent Strategy: Logical Obstacles to Action

Fear operates with a cunning strategy that persuades intelligent individuals to procrastinate. Instead of explicitly expressing opposition, it employs subtle and rational arguments to hinder progress. Fear employs phrases such as:

- "Delaying action until certainty is achieved."
- "Prioritising safety over potential risks."

- “Seeking additional information to make informed decisions.”

These rationalisations may sound familiar, as they effectively employ the voices of reason, responsibility, and logic to undermine the individual’s resolve.

The primary objective of fear is to prevent individuals from taking action. Remarkably, this strategy has proven effective in many instances.

Thinking vs. Overthinking

Let us establish a distinction at this juncture:

Thinking is the process of problem-solving and decision-making. It propels individuals forward. Overthinking, on the other hand, serves as an avoidance mechanism, resulting in a state of stagnation. Thinking possesses a clear objective and a linear progression. Overthinking, conversely, perpetuates an endless cycle of rumination. It is akin to fear engaging in repetitive mental activities.

A reliable indicator of crossing the threshold into overthinking is the persistence of a particular thought for an extended period, exceeding a day, without any tangible progress or action. Such behaviour does not constitute strategic thinking; rather, it is a manifestation of fear.

What Are You Really Afraid Of?

The uncomfortable truth is that you are not afraid of making a decision; you are afraid of the potential consequences of being wrong. You fear failure, embarrassment, social scrutiny, time wastage, and exacerbating the situation. In response, you attempt to overcome fear by repeatedly simulating scenarios in your mind. However, the only effective strategy is movement.

You Cannot Overthink Your Way Into Confidence

Overanalysis cannot lead to clarity, research cannot instil courage, and spreadsheets cannot drive action. If you desire to break free from stagnation, you must take action. You do not need to possess complete knowledge; it suffices to take the next step. Clarity emerges from action, confidence stems from evidence, and momentum arises from movement.

The Myth of Perfectionism

Let us clarify a misconception: perfectionism is not a virtue. It is not a matter of setting high standards, being meticulous, or striving for excellence. Perfectionism is, in fact, a manifestation of fear. It stems from the apprehension of judgment, failure, and the realisation that one may not meet unrealistic expectations. Consequently, individuals may adopt the self-perpetuating belief that perfection is a prerequisite for readiness.

This self-imposed limitation can be detrimental. By refusing to complete tasks, publish work, or engage in public speaking, individuals effectively shield themselves from criticism. However, this avoidance of criticism only serves to perpetuate self-criticism, preventing constructive feedback and personal growth.

Perfectionism as a Delay Strategy you may convince yourself that you are “working on it.” However, what you are truly doing is concealing your true intentions.

Allow me to be direct:

Perfectionism is a manifestation of fear, albeit disguised. It appears polished and impressive. Beneath the surface, it is merely insecurity whispering: "If it is not perfect, they will perceive me as a fraud." "If it is not perfect, I will fail." "If I make a mistake, I will never recover."

Consequently, your actions become: You revise. You procrastinate. You rewrite the email repeatedly. You never send it. All this while, the life you genuinely desire remains languishing in the drafts folder.

Perfect is a Myth

Seeking the truth? The concept of perfection is an illusion. The relentless pursuit of it is expending valuable time, energy, and opportunities. Allow me to share a revelation that resonates with every accomplished and self-assured individual: Achievement surpasses perfection. Authenticity surpasses refinement. Progress surpasses stagnation. The individuals who attain success are not those who possess an immaculate pitch, a flawless resume, or an impeccable plan. They are the ones who demonstrated courage to take action, even if their efforts were imperfect.

Unraveling the True Meaning Behind Perfectionism

When you express a desire for perfection, it is essential to examine the underlying motivations behind your actions.

The Desire for Recognition: When you state, "It's not ready yet," you may be intimating a fear of being perceived as inadequate.

The Fear of Criticism: When you express a desire to achieve the "best it can be," you might be harbouring apprehension about potential criticism.

The Procrastination of Action: When you declare, "I'll do it when it's perfect," you are essentially delaying the commencement of the task due to fear.

Recognising that perfectionism often disguises fear can empower you to break free from its shackles.

The Perilous Allure of "Needing to Be More Qualified"

Let us establish a clear understanding: You are not compelled to acquire additional certifications or degrees. You are not subject to the approval of others to pursue your aspirations.

However, I sense a persistent tendency within you to engage in self-deception. You frequently employ phrases such as: "I intend to pursue that role after completing one more course." "I merely require a slight increase in my practical experience." "Upon the completion of this program, I will be adequately prepared."
Do these statements resonate with you? Such assertions do not manifest humility; they do not constitute a strategic approach; rather, they are manifestations of fear masquerading as expertise.

Addressing Confidence and Qualifications: A Clarification

Allow me to pose a pertinent question: Are you genuinely unqualified?

Alternatively, are you merely apprehensive about presenting yourself and potentially not meeting the "ideal" criteria for the role? It is my observation, particularly among intelligent, capable, and high-performing individuals, that they often assume the necessity of accumulating credentials to acquire confidence.

However, confidence does not derive from a résumé; it emanates from action.

You Are Already More Qualified Than You Believe, skills are undoubtedly important, but if qualifications were the sole determining factor, the most confident individuals in the room would invariably be the most credentialed. However, this is not the case. How many times have you observed individuals with less experience, education, or accomplishments securing opportunities that align with your aspirations?

You have witnessed them enter the room, speak up, apply regardless, and ultimately be selected. The reason behind this is that they did not hesitate to feel qualified. Instead, they chose to project an aura of belongingness. And surprisingly, this approach fostered a sense of belief in their abilities among others.

The Qualification Illusion

Let us identify the underlying reason for your persistent procrastination:

You believe that acquiring a single additional document will finally quell the internal voice that asserts: "Your abilities are insufficient." "Who do you believe you are?" "They will discover your lack of belonging."

However, no certification on the planet can silence this voice. You cannot surpass your inner critic; you must outmanoeuvre it.

The World Rewards Visibility, Not Invisibility

Confidence makes you visible; credentials remain dormant on paper. Confidently entering a meeting and raising your hand distinguishes you from those who remain silent, hoping for recognition. You assert your ability to solve challenges, while credentials silently question their adequacy.

It is crucial to acknowledge that hiring, promotion, dating, investing, and betting are all predicated on the individual's presence and confidence rather than relying solely on a resume.

Confidence Equals Trust

When you approach situations with confidence, you establish trustworthiness. Trust in your initiative, problem-solving abilities, and reliability. Confidence does not imply omniscience; it signifies a willingness to learn, seek knowledge, and lead.

In the real world, individuals seek not a flawless track record but evidence of self-belief. After all, if you lack self-assurance, why should anyone else?

Credentials Ensure Eligibility, Confidence Secures the Position

This is paramount. Your qualifications may secure an initial opportunity, but confidence is the catalyst for securing the desired position. Furthermore, confidence is the driving force behind initiating the necessary actions. We have observed the following patterns:

- Jobs are awarded to those who actively seek them.
- Raises are granted to those who negotiate effectively.
- Attention is directed to those who embrace challenges, even if they experience trepidation.

Action surpasses perfection, and courage triumphs over caution.

Allow Me to Emphasise This Clearly

Confidence is a skill, not a inherent personality trait. Consequently, it is not something you are born with; rather, it is a skill that can be developed through consistent effort. This involves demonstrating presence, even in moments of apprehension, attempting to overcome uncertainty, and speaking despite trembling vocal cords.

There is no need to feign confidence; instead, it is essential to confront one's fears head-on. Confidence is not synonymous with fearlessness; rather, it is about taking action regardless of one's apprehension.

PART 2

THE TOOLS THAT SET YOU FREE

Okay, let's stop here for a second. If the first part of this book lit a fire under you, good.

If it made you uncomfortable—even better. That discomfort? It's not a sign you're broken. It's a sign you're waking up. Because you've spent enough of your life overthinking, doubting, stalling, shrinking. And now? You're done. Done playing small. Done letting fear call the shots. Done waiting for permission, validation, or "the right time."

How One Daily Practice Can Change Everything

Have you ever experienced one of those mornings where you wake up and your immediate thought is "No, not today. Not ready. I don't want to."

That was me.

Years ago, one morning, I found myself lying in bed, staring at the ceiling, evading my responsibilities. My marriage was in crisis, and I had recently lost my job. Bills piled up like a precarious game of Jenga.

I was trapped.

Not because I lacked knowledge of how to proceed, but because I lacked the motivation to take action. I was aware that I should rise and confront the day. However, the distinction between knowledge and action is profound.

Suddenly, an extraordinary occurrence transpired.

While watching a space documentary, I observed a rocket launch. As the countdown commenced, I realised that I could metaphorically launch myself out of bed, akin to a rocket. What if I abandoned my thoughts and simply moved?

Countdown to Transform Your Life

The following morning, as the alarm blared, I found myself counting down mentally.

5… 4… 3… 2… 1… Rise and shine.

With a clumsy and awkward motion, I threw off the covers and stood up. This simple yet effective technique proved to be a game-changer. I applied it repeatedly, from getting out of bed to making crucial calls, sending important emails, and breaking free from the cycle of overthinking that was diminishing my confidence. Whenever I felt about to hesitate or talk myself out of an opportunity, I would count down.

5, 4, 3, 2, 1—take action.

This practice transformed my life in profound ways.

The Science Behind this

Let us delve into the scientific basis of this practice, as it transcends mere motivational rhetoric. Neuroscience reveals that our brains have a limited time frame before they inhibit promising ideas. Neurological studies indicate that when an instinct arises to take action—speak up, take a risk, or submit an email—the prefrontal cortex becomes activated.

However, if no immediate action is taken within approximately countdown, the brain resorts to shutting down the idea due to fear, doubt, or rationalisations. This phenomenon is exemplified by the habit loop, a neural pattern that prioritises safety, silence, and delayed action.

The Countdown effectively interrupts this loop by employing a psychological strategy. It deceives the brain, engaging the prefrontal cortex, which is responsible for decision-making and concentration. Consequently, it effectively suppresses the automatic response of fear.

The True Power Lies Not in the Countdown, But in the Decision. It is imperative to clarify that this is not a magical solution or an instantaneous life hack. The power resides within you. The practice serves as a guiding instrument, enabling you to take action before your excuses manifest. Essentially, it functions as a bridge between theoretical knowledge and practical implementation.

Frankly, most of us do not require additional information; rather, we need the courage to act upon our existing knowledge.

Where You'll Use It (Spoiler: Everywhere)

You will use the Countdown practice in various situations, such as:

- When you are about to procrastinate speaking in a meeting.
- When your finger hovers over the "apply" button but hesitates.
- When you need to get out of bed and face your responsibilities.
- When the inner critic in your mind becomes vocal and questions your worth.

Now, let's proceed with the practice:

1. Begin counting down from five.

2. Continue counting down until you reach one.

The Importance of Action

It is crucial to note that confidence does not manifest before taking action; rather, it emerges as a consequence of action.

The Initial Challenges

The initial attempts at using the Countdown practice may feel unfamiliar and challenging. Your brain may resist, and your body may hesitate.

However, these initial difficulties are a positive sign. They indicate that you are breaking a pattern and choosing courage. As with any new habit, the practice strengthens with consistent use.

The Purpose of the Practice

The Countdown practice is not solely about willpower; it is primarily about breaking patterns. It is about providing yourself with the one essential element that has been lacking—not more information or qualifications, but simply more action. Therefore, when your intuition urges you to take action and your mind resists, it is essential to act promptly. Refrain from waiting, thinking, or negotiating. Simply count down:

Five
Four
Three
Two
One

Observe the outcomes and witness the transformative power of this simple yet effective practice.

The Neuroscience Behind the Countdown Practice

Have you ever wondered why it is so challenging to simply take action?

You desire to accomplish a task, are aware of its importance, yet an internal barrier hinders your progress. Suddenly, you find yourself scrolling through social media, indulging in snacks, or spiralling into distractions—anything but focusing on the one action that could propel your life forward.

This hesitation is not a sign of laziness or inadequacy; rather, it is a protective mechanism employed by your brain to safeguard you from potential risks.

Your Brain as a Survival Mechanism

Your brain's primary function is to sustain your life. It is indifferent to whether you achieve your goals, secure employment, express yourself, or pursue your dreams. Its sole concern is maintaining your safety and comfort.

Therefore, the moment you contemplate an uncertain or daunting task, your brain reacts with alarm. It floods your system with cortisol, the stress hormone, and initiates a series of internal dialogue:

"What if you fail?"

"What if you embarrass yourself?"
"Let us postpone this indefinitely…"

This hesitation you experience is merely your brain's attempt to protect you. However, it is crucial to understand that your brain struggles to distinguish between genuine physical threats and emotional ones.

To your brain, raising your hand in a meeting evokes the same level of apprehension as being pursued by a bear.

The Hesitation Habit Loop

Habit loops play a significant role in this phenomenon. The moment you hesitate, a loop is triggered.

The loop unfolds as follows:

Cue: An impulse arises, such as expressing an opinion, sending an email, or registering for an activity.
Craving: You anticipate the desired outcome, but fear emerges.
Response: You hesitate, engage in contemplation, and delay action.
Reward: Relief, as you have avoided potential risks. Your brain acknowledges your efforts.

Repeating this pattern reinforces the habit loop, making hesitation your default response. It perceives action as more perilous, leading to its perpetuation until it becomes an ingrained part of your behaviour.

The Impact of the Countdown Practice on the Brain

This is where the countdown practice comes into play.

The countdown practice generates a transformative effect on the brain.

When you count down—5, 4, 3, 2, 1—you activate the prefrontal cortex, the brain region responsible for decision-making, focus, and impulse control.

This action disrupts the default pattern and prevents your brain from overthinking the situation.

Consider it akin to flipping a switch:
From autopilot to conscious action.
From fear to focus.
From survival mode to action.

Your brain lacks time to rationalise against the instinctive response.

This process is swift, precise, and scientifically proven.

Why Five Seconds?

Because that is the window between thought and self-sabotage.

Studies in cognitive behavioural therapy reveal that there is a brief moment—a few seconds—between an instinct and the brain's tendency to undermine it with doubt.

Counting to ten indicates a delay in action, allowing hesitation to take control.

Counting to five, however, maintains control.

This is the critical juncture where confidence emerges—not from contemplation, but from action.

It's Not a Gimmick—It's a Pattern Interrupt

This psychological phenomenon is known as a pattern interrupt.

You are not relying on motivation, which is unreliable, nor are you engaging in a deep thought that can spiral into indecision.

Instead, you take control in the moment, utilising both your body and mind.

This is what makes the Countdown Practice so effective. It pierces through distractions and provides a physical anchor when your mind wanders.

The **Bottom Line**

Your brain's primary function is to protect you. Your role is to guide it.

The Countdown Practice empowers you to take control. It propels you out of autopilot, ignites your courage, and propels you forward before fear hinders your progress.

This approach is scientifically validated and grounded in brain science. Its effectiveness is undeniable.

Therefore, the next time you encounter hesitation, refrain from overthinking.

Simply count. And take action.

How Jessica Unknowingly Utilised It—And How You Can Intentionally Employ It

Remember Jessica?

The woman who attended a high-stakes strategy meeting, visibly anxious, experiencing physical distress, and desperately trying to convince herself once more that today was the day she would speak up?

She was unaware at the time, but when she finally raised her hand, she employed the Countdown practice.

Not intentionally, nor because she had read about it or practiced it. But because her body and mind reached a critical juncture, and she acted before her fear could paralyse her.

Here's what transpired: She experienced an urge. A subtle sensation in her gut that prompted her to speak.

Then came the hesitation.

Her inner critic emerged swiftly:
"Refrain from embarrassing yourself."
"What if your idea is flawed?"
"Your lack of seniority prevents you from contributing."

She felt herself shrinking. She glanced around the room, hoping someone else would speak up.

And then—she made a decision.

She did not contemplate; she did not analyse. She simply counted mentally.

5… 4… 3… 2… 1… and her hand rose.

It was not graceful; it was not even confident. But it was courageous.

When she finally spoke, she did not falter. The world did not end. People turned their attention to her. They listened attentively. She effectively conveyed her point.

And that small, imperfect, and shaky action ignited something within her.

She had acted before fear prevailed. That was the pivotal moment.

You Have Acted Before Fear Overwhelms You Admit it you have experienced similar moments. The call you made without deliberation. The text you sent before you could dissuade yourself. The time you stood up, walked away, or raised your hand because a deeper part of you moved faster than your fear.

You may not have labeled it the Countdown practice. But that is precisely what you did: you acted before your mind could hinder you.

Now, envision the ability to do so intentionally.

Not merely in rare instances of spontaneous courage… But every time you needed to overcome self-doubt, hesitation, or fear.

How to Implement It Intentionally

Here's how this works in practical situations:

1. You perceive it—the instinct, the impulse, the "I should do this" nudge.
2. You recognise the hesitation—fear disguised as your brain's resistance.
3. Count Down.

Out loud or silently, count down from five to one.

4. Take Action.

Say it, do it, hit send, walk in, raise your hand, and break the pattern.

That's it.

You don't need to feel ready, confident, or have a plan.

You just need to move before fear takes over.

Jessica's Secret Weapon Can Be Yours

Jessica's instinctive actions can now be done deliberately. The difference between staying stuck in your head and actually doing the things that build confidence lies in this. Confidence is earned by doing scary, brave, and uncomfortable things, one tiny action at a time. The countdown practice serves as your launchpad.

So, the next time you feel hesitation, don't wait.

Catch it, count it down, and go.

The life you want—the boldness, the respect, the opportunities lies beyond the countdown of courage.

Count Down, Take Action, Change Your Life

Let's simplify the process.

Do you want change? Confidence? To stop overthinking and start living authentically?

The truth is: It begins with the countdown.

Count Down

Feel the hesitation, the tightness in your chest, the flicker of doubt, the moment when you almost take action but then hesitate.

Stop right there.

Begin counting. 5… 4… 3… 2… 1…

It may sound deceptively simple, but here's the key: You are not counting for amusement; you are counting to gain control. Each time you countdown, you interrupt the habit loop that keeps you stuck. You override the autopilot switch and activate your prefrontal cortex

—the region of your brain responsible for making decisions and taking action.

This is neuroscience in action.

Take Action

Here is the practice: Upon reaching "1," take action.

Speak the desired action. Step forward. Raise your hand. Close the laptop. Get out of bed. Hit "send." Engage in any activity, even if it is small. Do not wait for readiness or confidence. Simply move forward.

Action builds confidence; not the other way around.

With each action, you teach your brain a new pattern: "I am the kind of person who shows up." "I am the kind of person who tries." "I no longer let fear dictate my choices."

This is how you cultivate identity-level confidence—not through contemplation or wishful thinking, but through action.

Change Your Life

This may sound grandiose, but it is not. When you consistently demonstrate presence in the small moments the challenging conversations, the gruelling workouts, the difficult decisions you transform the broader perspective of your life. This is what Jessica accomplished, what I achieved, and what millions of individuals have done through this practice. The Countdown Practice may not eliminate your problems, but it will provide you with the fortitude to confront them directly.

This transformation has a profound impact.

Conclusion

Therefore, the takeaway is:

In the face of uncertainty, hesitation, or indecision, it is crucial to avoid overthinking and procrastination. Instead, adopt a proactive approach by counting down and taking immediate action. This simple yet effective strategy can transform your life and lead to positive changes.

Real-World Application: Meetings, Relationships, Health, Creativity

Understanding the Countdown Practice is one step; applying it in real-world scenarios is another. Whether in a meeting, a conversation, or facing a blank page, this technique can be invaluable when courage falters.

In Meetings: Speak Before Overthinking

Imagine you are in a meeting, armed with a solid idea. However, you begin to spiral into self-doubt, questioning its validity and fearing rejection. This hesitation can paralyse you and prevent you from expressing your thoughts.

Instead of succumbing to fear, acknowledge the urge to speak. Begin counting down from five to one, lean in, raise your hand, and initiate the conversation. Even if your voice trembles or your heart races, the act of speaking is crucial.

This approach fosters recognition, advancement, and respect, demonstrating that bravery and initiative are more important than intelligence alone.

In Relationships: Express Your Needs

Silence can be the most detrimental factor in relationships. It is essential to communicate openly and honestly, addressing any concerns or issues promptly.

Refrain from expressing your true feelings, avoiding challenging questions, or setting clear boundaries.

It is that moment when your intuition urges you to speak up, while your rational mind hesitates.

Practice this technique.

The next time your partner's words hurt, you need to express your needs, or you finally decide to share your true feelings, employ the 5-4-3-2-1 method. Speak.

Perfection is not essential; honesty is crucial.

True intimacy arises from courage, not comfort.

In Health: Act Before Negotiation

The alarm sounds. You are aware that you should rise. You desire to visit the gym, take a walk, or avoid the donut.

However, your mind engages in its morning monologue:
"Just a few more minutes."
"I will commence tomorrow."
"I am too fatigued."

Silence the internal dialogue.

The practice provides you with a tool to act before your mind dissuades you.

Upon hearing the alarm, employ the 5-4-3-2-1 method. Rise.

When you notice the chips and recall your objective, employ the 5-4-3-2-1 method to walk away.

When your shoes are near the door and you lack motivation, employ the 5-4-3-2-1 method to move.

Discipline does not necessitate motivation; it requires a moment of action. Countdown. That is the essence.

In Creativity: Overcoming the Blank Page

You aspire to write a book, commence a podcast, or launch a business. However, you stare at the screen and contemplate:
"I am not prepared."
"Who am I to undertake such a task?"
"What if the outcome is unsatisfactory?"

It is imperative to acknowledge that initial efforts may be subpar. This is the inherent nature of the process.

Nevertheless, creativity does not require permission; it demands action.

The Countdown Practice: A Powerful Tool for Overcoming Procrastination

The Countdown Practice is a versatile tool that can be applied to various aspects of life, from personal development to professional success. It is a simple yet effective method that can help individuals overcome procrastination and achieve their goals.

The Process:

1. **Begin with a Countdown:** Start by writing down the first sentence of a great work.
2. Open Your Laptop: Open your laptop and prepare to make a call.
3. **Take Action:** Take immediate action without hesitation.

The Power of the Countdown:

The Countdown Practice is a powerful tool that can be used in various situations, such as meetings, conversations, workouts, making difficult decisions, forming new habits, and setting ambitious goals. Whenever you feel hesitant or uncertain, take advantage of the Countdown Practice to take action.

The Decision:

The key to the Countdown Practice's effectiveness lies in the decision you make at the end of each countdown. Will you succumb to fear and procrastinate, or will you overcome it and move forward?

Overcoming Stagnation:

The Countdown Practice can be particularly effective when you feel stuck or unmotivated. By counting down and taking immediate action, you can break free from these barriers and transform your life. you'll speak. And that's what matters. That's how people get noticed, promoted, respected. Not by being the smartest. But by being the one brave enough to show up.

In Relationships: Say What Needs to Be Said

You know what ruins more relationships than anything?

Silence.

Not saying what's on your heart. Not asking the hard questions. Not drawing the boundaries you know you need. It's that moment when your gut screams, "Speak up," and your brain whispers, "Better not."

Use the practice.

Next time your partner says something that stings, or you need to ask for what you need, or finally say what's true for you?

5-4-3-2-1. Speak.

It doesn't have to be perfect. It just has to be honest. Because real intimacy doesn't come from comfort—it comes from courage.

It's One Practice. A Million Uses.

The Countdown Practice is a Swiss Army knife for your brain. Meetings. Conversations. Workouts. Hard choices. New habits. Big goals. Anywhere there's hesitation, there's a moment to use it.

The question is: Will you let fear lead, or will you move anyway?

Next time you feel stuck?

Count down. Take action. Change your life.

How to Stop Overthinking and Start Taking Action

Overthinking feels like productivity — but it's really disguised paralysis. Studies by Susan Nolen-Hoeksema (2000) and more recently by Ethan Kross (2021) show that rumination doesn't lead to clarity; it leads to stress, indecision, and burnout. Our brains trick us into believing that if we just "think a little longer," we'll be more prepared — but action is what creates momentum, not endless planning. Cognitive-behavioral research confirms that small, deliberate steps interrupt the loop of mental noise and rewire the brain for forward motion. This chapter is your practical guide to getting out of your head — and back into your life.

Let me ask you something. How many times have you said you wanted to do something—speak up, work out, apply for the job, start the thing—and then sat around thinking about it instead of actually doing it?

You lacked a plan, did not require more time, nor did you need to "get ready."

You were simply preoccupied with your thoughts.

And that is where dreams ultimately perish.

The Truth: Thinking Isn't the Issue—Overthinking Is

Thinking is beneficial. It is essential for planning, problem-solving, and decision-making.

However, overthinking is akin to wearing yoga pants in fear. It may appear productive, but it is actually a form of avoidance.

Overthinking manifests in the following manner:
"What is the most effective approach to commence?"
"What if I encounter failure?"
"Perhaps I should conduct further research…"
"I will commence on Monday. Alternatively, next month. Or perhaps next year."

The internal voice in your mind does not intend to assist you. Instead, it seeks to safeguard you—from risk, failure, and embarrassment.

However, it is crucial to acknowledge that confidence is not acquired through thinking alone. It is cultivated through action.

Conversely, the longer you remain confined within your thoughts, the more pronounced fear becomes.

Jessica's Turning Point

Let us revisit Jessica's situation.

Following her initial meeting, where she finally expressed herself, she faced a critical juncture. She could succumb to overthinking, contemplating whether her actions were appropriate, if she appeared foolish, or whether she should follow up via email. Alternatively, she could capitalise on the momentum and continue attending meetings.

She chose action.

At the next meeting, she spoke again. In the meeting that followed, she took the lead in presenting her pitch. A few weeks later, her manager recognised her as a rising star.

This recognition was not attributed to her acquiring a new degree or developing a fearless demeanour. Rather, it was a consequence of her proactive approach.

She ceased being ensnared in the cycle of excessive thinking and embarked on a series of courageous actions.

The Power of Movement

What many individuals overlook is the transformative effect of movement on overthinking.

When you engage in physical activity or take any form of action, you activate the prefrontal cortex, the brain region responsible for decision-making. This process enables you to break free from autopilot and assume control.

Consider this analogy: Your thoughts are akin to the tracks on a train. However, your actions represent the switch that determines the train's direction.

Therefore, when you perceive yourself spiralling into overthinking, such as contemplating hypothetical scenarios, it is counterproductive to attempt to outsmart the situation.

Instead, take action. Stand up, walk outside, open an email, record a message, make a call, raise your hand, or simply express your need for a conversation.

The specific action may vary, but the key is to disrupt the repetitive pattern of thought.

The most effective strategy for achieving this is to cease thinking altogether and commence moving.

The Confidence Loop

To truly comprehend the construction of genuine confidence, consider the following process:

Take Action: The foundation of confidence lies in taking proactive steps.
Gather Evidence: These actions provide tangible evidence that reinforces belief.
Build Belief: Belief, in turn, strengthens the motivation to continue taking action.
Reinforce Action: The cycle continues, with belief reinforcing action, and action reinforcing belief.

It is important to note that confidence does not emerge overnight; rather, it is cultivated through consistent action. Even if the journey is challenging, incremental progress is crucial. Embrace the imperfections and allow your voice to tremble as you embark on this transformative process.

Confidence is not a byproduct of success; rather, it is a consequence of consistent motion.

The "One Brave Move" Challenge

Today's challenge is to take a single, courageous action. Refrain from overanalyzing the situation or creating an extensive plan. Select one aspect that evokes a sense of apprehension and proceed with action.

For instance, if you aspire to establish a blog, compose the initial sentence. If networking intimidates you, dispatch a single message. If you feel overlooked in meetings, contribute once. If you desire to improve your fitness, undertake a single walk.

Embrace the concept of a single, courageous step. That is the essence of the challenge.

Set a timer and proceed with the countdown: 5, 4, 3, 2, 1.

You will experience a surge of exhilaration and momentum, accompanied by a profound sense of accomplishment.

This sensation represents confidence, not an artificial, polished form. It is a genuine, earned confidence.

Once you attain this confidence, you will naturally desire to engage in further actions.

Final Thought: Clarity Arises from Action

Many individuals procrastinate by seeking clarity before taking action. However, I have discovered that clarity does not originate from contemplation; rather, it emerges from action.

Identifying one's strengths, self-awareness, and aspirations is not achieved through passive journaling. Instead, it is cultivated through experiential living. Therefore, it is crucial to cease overthinking, refrain from waiting for perfection, and dispel the notion of inadequacy.

You possess sufficient readiness.

Five-Four-Three-Two-One Method: Take Action

Begin by implementing the Five-Four-Three-Two-One method to initiate action.

Confidence will eventually catch up with you.

Momentum Overcomes Motivation

Contrary to popular belief, motivation is not a reliable catalyst for progress.

Society has conditioned us to associate motivation with the prerequisite of readiness, inspiration, and energy before taking action.

However, the truth is that action is the prerequisite for motivation.

Momentum holds greater significance than motivation because it is a tangible force that can be cultivated and built upon. Once momentum is established, even challenging tasks become more manageable.

Jessica's Remark: Overcoming Initial Fear

Later, during her tenure as a mentor to junior team members, Jessica shared an insightful experience.

She recounted, "The initial meeting was fraught with apprehension. My heart raced, and I grappled with the prospect of choking. Nevertheless, I employed a countdown technique and delivered my speech. Subsequently, a profound transformation occurred."

Jessica did not feel courageous before taking action; rather, she felt courageous afterward.

The subsequent meeting presented a slight ease, not due to a revelation or an instantaneous transformation, but because momentum was in her favour.

This principle encapsulates the essence of effective action.

The Power of Action: Overcoming Procrastination

Procrastination can be a persistent challenge, but it is not insurmountable. Instead of waiting for inspiration to strike, it is crucial to take action.

Motivation is an ephemeral state, akin to a wave that ebbs and flows. However, momentum is a tangible decision that can propel us forward.

Rather than passively awaiting inspiration, we should actively initiate our goals. This can be achieved by taking small, consistent steps, such as sending an email, making a phone call, or speaking up. Each action, no matter how insignificant, contributes to building momentum.

The brain's reward system plays a pivotal role in this process. When we engage in any form of action, we release dopamine, a neurotransmitter that reinforces positive experiences and encourages repetition. This dopamine release generates forward energy and desire, propelling us to continue our efforts.

However, the benefits of action are diminished when we remain stagnant, waiting for inspiration to strike. The key is to recognise that the brain cannot distinguish between significant and minor actions. Momentum is not contingent upon the magnitude of our efforts; it is solely dependent on our consistent progress.

Therefore, rather than dwelling on the possibility of inspiration, we should focus on taking action and building momentum. Every step, no matter how small, contributes to our overall progress and helps us overcome procrastination.

Your Role: Initiate and Persevere

Your primary responsibility is to take action promptly. Your brain may attempt to maintain a sense of security through meticulous planning, urging you to overprepare, meticulously analyse, and await motivation.

However, it is crucial to disregard these internal pressures and commence with small, scrappy, and even fearful steps. Simply start.

By doing so, you will generate the momentum necessary not only to initiate a task but also to sustain progress.

The Psychology of Micro-Decisions

If you aspire for significant life transformations, it is essential to focus on the micro-decisions that shape your trajectory. These decisions occur in fleeting moments, such as the split second when your alarm sounds and you choose to extend the snooze or rise promptly. In the pause before speaking, you must decide whether to remain silent or convey the truth. In the interval between perceiving an opportunity and either embracing it or acknowledging your readiness, you must make a choice.

Confidence is not forged through substantial achievements; rather, it is cultivated through repeated, small choices made over time.

Life Occurs in Five-Second Windows

Based on my personal experience and extensive coaching of thousands, I have come to understand that there are micro-moments throughout the day that determine the trajectory of your life.

Consider the second your name is called in a meeting, where your brain instinctively resists speaking, while your gut urges you to contribute. Think about the moment you encounter the individual you have long desired to approach, and your feet become paralysed. Reflect on the unsent email that languishes in your drafts.

It is not the grand speeches that transform lives; rather, it is the moment when you make a conscious decision to accept an opportunity.

These micro-decisions may not appear life-altering in the present, but they possess transformative power. Each time you choose courage over comfort, even in the smallest of ways, you are rewriting your brain's programming. You are casting a vote for the future version of yourself.

Why Your Brain Fights It

Let us delve into the intricacies of the human mind.

Your brain is meticulously designed to ensure your survival, not necessarily your happiness, fulfilment, or courage. It is solely focused on maintaining your life.

Consequently, your brain is constantly scanning for potential risks. To your brain, risk no longer encompasses physical dangers such as being chased by a bear. Instead, it encompasses the fear of judgment, failure, embarrassment, and discomfort.

As a result, in every micro-decision you make, your brain introduces hesitation. It prompts you to pause, consider the matter further, or delay action.

Hesitation, in essence, hinders the development of confidence.

This is precisely why the Countdown Practice proves effective. It disrupts the hesitation loop, allowing your instinct to take precedence over your fear.

The Micro Wins that Build Mega Confidence

Here is a revelation that Jessica did not comprehend until we elucidated it further:

The moment she raised her hand was a mere micro-decision.

However, it was preceded by ten other such decisions.

She had entered that meeting with a slightly taller posture. She had refrained from using her phone, opting instead to engage in face-to-face interactions. She had maintained eye contact with others. She had decided against overthinking her comment and simply offering it.

Each of these decisions was a micro-decision.

The cumulative effect of these micro-decisions was the catalyst for rewiring her confidence. It transformed her internal dialogue from self-doubt to self-assurance.

Confidence is not an instantaneous phenomenon; it is a muscle that requires consistent effort. Each micro-decision you make contributes to the development of this muscle, akin to a series of repetitions.

What to Do with This?

Stop overthinking your significant goals, waiting for the opportune moment, and begin practicing micro-courage.

Pick up the phone instead of procrastinating, send the message, ask the question, or put your name in the hat.

Make one micro-decision at a time.

This is how you build momentum, create confidence, and transform your life.

Building Confidence Through Action First, Feelings Later

Contrary to popular belief, confidence is not a feeling; it is a decision.

You have been taught to pursue a feeling—as if one day you will awaken with unwavering confidence, akin to a superhero in a Marvel movie. However, this approach is flawed.

Confidence does not manifest before you undertake the daunting task; it emerges after you do.

The anticipation, belief, or certainty you seek is not the catalyst; it is the reward.

Confidence is Earned Through Action

You do not "think" your way into confidence; you earn it, gradually, by taking action, particularly when you feel unprepared.

Consider this: each time you take action despite fear, hesitation, nervousness, or doubt, you are constructing the foundation of your confidence. Initially, it may be imperceptible, and you may not even perceive a difference. Nevertheless, it is occurring.

For instance, Jessica lacked confidence when she raised her hand. She felt apprehensive. However, after speaking? After the room responded positively and someone acknowledged her point? That moment solidified her nervous system. It conveyed, “You persevered, and it was successful.”

In essence, you have completed another rep in the confidence gym.

Why You’re Waiting—and Why It’s a Limiting Factor

Have you ever uttered the following statement:

“I will take action when I feel more confident.”

This sentiment is likely familiar to you. However, it is crucial to understand that this approach is counterproductive. It is akin to asserting that you will commence an exercise regimen once you attain a desired level of fitness.

The reality is that confidence does not precede action. Rather, action precedes confidence.

Refrain from relinquishing your power to a feeling that has not yet earned its rightful place.

Your Brain’s Reward Mechanism for Movement

When you engage in challenging or uncomfortable activities, your brain responds with a sense of accomplishment. This triggers the release of dopamine, the neurotransmitter associated with a sense of achievement and motivation. Subsequently, your brain reinforces this association, encouraging you to repeat the action.

This process is instrumental in developing genuine confidence. By training your brain to associate movement with safety, pride, and power, you can build a more robust sense of self-assurance.

Each time you confront a vulnerable situation and successfully overcome it, you reinforce a fundamental truth that can transform your life:

"I possess the ability to handle challenging tasks."

This realisation is attainable, but it requires self-proof.

Embarking on a Journey of Self-Discovery: A Proactive Approach

It is not necessary to undertake monumental tasks such as delivering a TED Talk tomorrow or quitting your job to pursue your dream business. However, it is crucial to adopt the persona of the individual you aspire to become.

This persona embodies courage, not merely confidence. It demonstrates the willingness to speak up even when faced with apprehension.

A guiding principle is that emotions follow actions. Therefore, it is advisable to act bravely rather than waiting for feelings to arise. By taking proactive steps, the emotions will naturally follow suit.

Case Studies: Transforming Lives through Strategic Decision-Making

To substantiate the effectiveness of this approach, let us consider the transformative journeys of three individuals who made decisive choices that profoundly impacted their lives.

These individuals are not celebrities or influencers with idealised portrayals on social media. They are ordinary people with common challenges such as doubts, chaotic mornings, overdue bills, and fears that seemed insurmountable.

However, they consistently made strategic decisions, one at a time. Their lives underwent a remarkable transformation, not due to a preconceived master plan, but through their unwavering movement and proactive actions.

Case 1: Maria - The Silent Contributor

Maria was an exceptional marketing professional in her mid-thirties, renowned for her brilliance in her field. However, she exhibited a persistent tendency to remain silent during meetings, despite possessing the knowledge to contribute.

Each meeting presented a challenge for Maria. She would replay her thoughts in her mind, meticulously verify their accuracy, and yet, she would choose to remain silent. Over time, her colleagues began to cease seeking her input.

A pivotal moment occurred when a junior hire presented Maria's own innovative idea, which was met with overwhelming approval from the supervisor. This experience left Maria deeply shaken, not with anger towards the newcomer, but with profound self-criticism for her reluctance to express herself.

Determined to overcome this obstacle, Maria adopted a new approach. She resolved to take a five-second pause before speaking, acknowledging the potential discomfort of doing so.

Initially, Maria felt ill-prepared, but she persisted in her resolve. She counted down from five to one, and in the midst of a brainstorming session, she found the courage to speak up.

This pivotal moment paved the way for a follow-up question and subsequently, a leadership opportunity. Six months later, Maria was promoted and now mentors other women on asserting their voices.

In a candid reflection, Maria emphasised, "Confidence did not find me; I constructed it through consistent effort, one uncomfortable sentence at a time."

Case 2: Kevin - The Stuck Dreamer

Kevin epitomised the archetype of an idea-generating individual, possessing notebooks brimming with business plans, app concepts, and startup strategies.

However, when it came to translating these ideas into tangible actions, Kevin faced significant challenges. He attributed his inaction to a perceived lack of time, resources, and thorough research. In reality, Kevin harboured deep-seated fears of failure, embarrassment, and the perception of inadequacy.

One day, while browsing online rather than dedicating time to his pitch deck, Kevin stumbled upon a video that resonated with him. The video introduced the concept of the Countdown Practice, which resonated with his aspirations.

Kevin made a conscious decision to shift his focus from planning to action. He resolved to take one decision at a time, moving forward with a determined mindset. His initial action was a bold email to a former coworker, expressing his interest in discussing his app idea. The recipient responded promptly, inviting a meeting within 15 minutes.

Kevin's proactive approach eliminated the need for waiting for a website or business card. By taking a single action, he successfully gained access to a potential collaborator.

Within a year, Kevin achieved significant milestones, including the development of a functional beta, the acquisition of a cofounder, and the presence of actual users. This success was not attributed to fearlessness, but rather to the acquisition of a valuable skill in navigating and overcoming fear, one decision at a time.

Case 3: Deena's Health Reset

Deena had exhausted every diet, reset, and Monday-morning resolution.

She experienced weight fluctuations, abandoned workout plans, and succumbed to decision fatigue. Her attempts to overhaul her lifestyle were met with disinterest and abandonment.

One morning, confronted with her self-loathing, Deena uttered, "I cannot continue this self-sabotage."

Recalling a podcast revelation, she realised that confidence stems from action, not contemplation.

She made a simple change: drinking water before coffee.

Building on this foundation, Deena implemented incremental improvements: walking around the block, packing lunches instead of ordering takeout, and incorporating a five-minute morning stretch.

Each small decision stacked upon the previous, transforming Deena's self-perception from failure to consistency and trustworthiness.

Six months later, Deena achieved a remarkable weight loss of 40 pounds. Moreover, her self-respect, energy, and momentum soared.

Your Turn

These anecdotes are not extraordinary; they represent the micro-decisions made by individuals like you. They did not await readiness or motivation; they commenced where they were, utilising their resources, and progressed.

One action at a time.

Knowledge of the destination is not essential; the first step is sufficient.

If they succeeded, you can too.

How to Build Confidence That Sticks

Real confidence doesn't come from repeating affirmations — it comes from stacking evidence. Research by Albert Bandura (1997), the father of self-efficacy theory, shows that lasting confidence is built through "mastery experiences" — small wins that prove to yourself, over time, that you can handle more than you thought. Harvard psychologist Amy Cuddy (2015) adds that behavior shapes belief: when you act boldly, your brain begins to catch up. Confidence, then, is not a personality trait — it's a habit. In this chapter, we'll dismantle the myth of being born confident, and learn how to build it piece by piece, action by action, until it becomes who you are.

Let me give it to you straight: Confidence is not something you're born with. It's not something only loud, extroverted, polished people get. It's not even something you "find" one day.

Confidence is a habit, akin to brushing your teeth, checking your phone first thing in the morning, or pouring coffee without conscious thought.

Confidence can become automatic only if cultivated as a habit.

To achieve this, cease chasing the feeling of confidence and instead, implement the actions that generate it consistently. Repeat these actions until they become second nature.

Let's analyse this process:

Habits govern our lives. Therefore, let us make confidence one of them.

As you likely already know, the brain thrives on patterns. The frequency of repetition facilitates the ease of repetition.

For instance, you don't consciously think about driving home from work; your brain executes the program automatically.

Similarly, your fear, hesitation, second-guessing, and impulse to shrink and remain silent are habits. You've repeated them so many times that they feel like your personality.

However, the good news is that you can introduce new habits.

Confidence is not a magical solution; it is muscle memory.

The Formation of Habits: A Comprehensive Explanation

Habits are formed through a cyclical process involving a cue, a routine, and a reward. For instance, before a meeting, you may feel nervous (cue), leading you to remain silent (routine) and avoid discomfort (reward). This response reinforces the habit of avoiding risk, even if it entails sacrificing your voice, visibility, and personal growth.

Conversely, when you feel nervous, you can counter this by counting backward (5-4-3-2-1) and speaking anyway (routine). This action interrupts the fear loop and activates your prefrontal cortex, your action centre. By taking the smallest courageous step, such as speaking up, raising your hand, making a call, publishing a post, or entering the room, you reinforce your confidence.

Positive reinforcement, such as smiling, fist pumping, or affirming your accomplishment, accelerates the brain's ability to internalise these habits. Repetition is key to building confidence, and each successful action contributes to its consolidation.

The Daily Path to Confidence

Consider the following practical approach to cultivating daily confidence:

Rise and Shine: Upon waking, resist the urge to scroll through social media. Instead, engage in a five-step countdown to get out of bed and move.

Embrace Your Ideas: At work, when an idea arises, resist the temptation to procrastinate. Implement a five-step countdown to articulate your thoughts.

Conquer Tough Conversations: In challenging conversations, resist the inclination to retreat. Engage in a five-step countdown to breathe deeply and express your feelings.

Prioritise Self-Care: When faced with physical demands, such as skipping a walk, resist the urge to indulge in comfort. Implement a five-step countdown to put on your shoes and take action.

Each moment you choose courage over comfort constitutes a vote for the version of yourself you are developing. These votes accumulate rapidly, leading to significant transformation.

From Hesitation to Habitual Confidence

Allow me to share the experience of one of my coaching clients, Taylor.

Taylor exhibited a tendency to approach tasks with hesitation, often opting for the "almost" path. She refrained from asking for a raise, starting a podcast, or expressing her true feelings in her relationships.

Seeking professional guidance, Taylor identified her habits as the root cause of her challenges. She recognised that her habitual approach to hesitation, playing small, and waiting for "ready" moments hindered her progress.

To address this, we implemented a rewiring strategy. Whenever Taylor felt doubt, she would engage in a five-step countdown to take action. Similarly, whenever she overthought a situation, she would send an email, and whenever she felt the urge to retreat, she would make an effort to be present.

A year later, Taylor has transformed her mindset. She no longer hesitates; she takes action confidently. Confidence has become an integral part of her daily routine.

You Can Build It Too

Pay attention: this is not about becoming someone you are not.

It is about finally accessing the you that has been concealed beneath fear, hesitation, and erroneous programming.

You possess all the necessary resources. You have simply been operating under incorrect habits.

Therefore, commence today.

Begin modestly.

Begin purposefully.

For when you train your mind to act, not retract—when you establish courage as your default setting—that is when confidence ceases to be a mere facade…

…and transforms into something tangible.

Daily Actions That Rewire Your Brain for Boldness

Do you aspire to feel bolder? Excellent. Then cease waiting for boldness to strike unexpectedly.

Boldness is not a fleeting emotion. It is a muscle.

And just as any muscle, it is developed through consistent use. Every single day.

One aspect that is often overlooked is that your brain is wired to prioritise safety over success. It is attempting to avoid risk, embarrassment, exertion, and rejection. Consequently, whenever you even contemplate undertaking an action outside your comfort zone—such as speaking up, requesting additional responsibilities, or attempting something novel—your brain responds with resistance.

This resistance does not stem from a lack of capability. Rather, it arises from unfamiliarity.

Desire to alter this?

You must make boldness familiar.

This is achieved by repeating bold behaviour until it becomes routine.

The Confidence Circuit Workout

I am not referring to meditating atop mountains or creating vision boards with glitter pens.

I am discussing simple, practical exercises that you can undertake today—before dinner, before that meeting, even while brushing your teeth.

Each of these small actions rewires your brain to anticipate courage from you, not fear. Courage.

Daily Boldness Workout

1. Interrupt Hesitation (with 5-4-3-2-1 Method)

Feel the hesitation—you know you do. That brief pause before action. This is your opportunity. Count backward: 5-4-3-2-1. Then take action.

Not later. Not "after contemplation." Now.

Interrupt the habit of waiting, and your brain trains to act rather than freeze.

2. Engage in Challenging Actions Daily

Embrace one small risk. That is it.

Speak in meetings. Request your needs. Decline offers when you would usually accept. Introduce yourself. Present your pitch. Share your content.

Avoid extreme actions. Just undertake something your fear would strongly oppose—and do it anyway.

This is how you build boldness: one step at a time.

3. Celebrate Every Act of Courage (Even the Small Ones)

Your brain perceives the pattern: action, survival, and positive feelings.

Acknowledge each courageous act.

Express it aloud: "That was bold." Smile. Celebrate your accomplishment.

You are programming your brain to crave courage, not fear.

4. Identify and Confront Your Inner Critic

The moment you hear the voice—"Who do you believe you are?" or "You are not prepared"—name it.

Laugh at it. Minimise its impact. You cannot negotiate with fear; you must overcome it with action.

Interrupt the self-doubt, then act as boldness would.

5. Visualise Your Actions, Not Thoughts

At night or upon waking, visualise yourself performing the bold action.

Embrace uncertainty and lack of bravery. Simply take the necessary steps.

Your brain, akin to a film editor, becomes influenced by repeated images. Begin playing bold footage.

6. Surround Yourself with Action-Oriented Individuals

This aspect is more significant than you may realise.

If your colleagues are all waiting for readiness, you will inevitably wait as well.

However, when you begin watching, texting, reading, listening to individuals who move, take risks, and speak truthfully, you inevitably absorb their energy.

Confidence is contagious, as is playing small. Therefore, it is crucial to select your tribe judiciously.

habits, done consistently, to rewire your brain.

Because here's the truth: Confidence isn't built in the big moments. It's built in the small ones—when no one's watching. When you decide to be the kind of person who acts.

And the more often you do that? The less fear gets a vote. The more confidence gets to run the show.

Morning Confidence Rituals

(Because how you start your day is how you live your life.)

Let me ask you something real quick: When your alarm goes off, what's the first thing you do?

If your answer sounds like, "hit snooze, scroll Instagram, dread everything," then I want you to hear this loud and clear:

You're not starting your day. You're reacting to it. And that's a problem. Because confidence doesn't live in reactivity. Confidence lives in intention.

If you want to be more confident, you've got to prime yourself for it before the world even gets a chance to throw its noise at you.

And no, I'm not going to tell you to wake up at 5 AM, journal for an hour, and make kale smoothies while chanting affirmations.

I'm going to give you something better: A short, powerful morning ritual that builds mental strength, clarity, and courage—on autopilot.

The Morning Confidence Ritual (7 Minutes or Less)

Confidence is a skill that can be developed through consistent practice. The most effective time to practice is first thing in the morning, before your doubts arise and hinder your progress.

The Ritual:

1. **Rise Promptly:** Avoid snoozing, negotiating, or engaging in drama. The first promise you make and keep each day should be to yourself.

2. **Mirror Self-Affirmation:** Engage in a brief self-affirmation, such as "I am the kind of person who…" Fill in the blank with the identity you wish to embody. For instance, "I am the kind of person who speaks up," "I am the kind of person who takes action," or "I am the kind of person who gets things done."

3. **Activate Positive Reinforcement:** This simple gesture activates dopamine, elevates your mood, and reprograms your brain to support your goals. Remember, the purpose is not to enhance your appearance, but rather to train your brain to treat yourself with self-assurance.

Why Does This Matter?

Your brain is receptive to your thoughts and beliefs. By reinforcing your identity, you diminish the resistance you experience when it is time to act in accordance with your self-perception.

This mental exercise serves as a confidence-building push-up.

4. **One Bold Move—Planned in Advance**

Prioritise a single action that will challenge, develop, and bolster your confidence for the day. This action should not be overwhelming; it is sufficient to begin.

Consider options such as making a phone call, posting a video, expressing your true thoughts, or requesting what you need. Choose one action, write it down, and complete it before noon.

Momentum precedes motivation; therefore, initiating a small action can lead to significant progress.
e. Just a decision. A few simple actions. Repeated daily.

You don't rise to the level of your goals. You fall to the level of your habits.

Let your morning be the launchpad for boldness—not another replay of hesitation.

Win the First 10 Minutes, Win the Day

Look, I'm going to say this the way it needs to be said:

You don't need a miracle morning. You need a moment of control.

That moment? It's right when you wake up.

The first 10 minutes of your day are either training your brain to take charge—or letting fear and distraction take the wheel before you've even brushed your teeth.

And here's the brutal truth no one talks about:

Most people lose the day before they've even started it.

They reach for their phone. They check the news. They scroll. They react. And they wonder why they feel anxious, behind, or unmotivated.

It's not a mystery. It's momentum—in the wrong direction.

The True Nature of Your First 10 Minutes

Upon waking, your brain enters a state of vulnerability, with the prefrontal cortex, responsible for decision-making, experiencing a state of grogginess. Conversely, your subconscious patterns remain fully active.

The initial 10 minutes, akin to wet cement, shape your mindset. The actions, thoughts, and emotions you experience during this period establish the foundation for the remainder of your day.

You have two choices: succumb to habitual patterns that limit your growth or make a conscious decision to take control. This pivotal choice serves as the bedrock for the rest of your day.

Achieving perfection is not the objective; rather, it is about intentionality.

The Three Obstacles That Derail Your First 10 Minutes

It is crucial to acknowledge the following challenges:

1. **Snoozing:** This action trains your brain to procrastinate. Each time you snooze, you reinforce hesitation.
2. **Reaching for the phone:** This act outsources your priorities. The moment you check messages, you relinquish control over your emotional state to external influences.
3. **Mental downloading of the to-do list:** This process builds stress before momentum. It is unnecessary to dwell on every task; focus on taking action that propels you forward.

Inverting the Process

How can you reverse this pattern?

The Simple Fix: Establish a 10-Minute Power Zone

Avoid overcomplicating the process. You do not require 15 steps. Instead, focus on moving with intention and prioritising momentum over passivity.

Consider the following scenario for achieving those 10 minutes:

Immediately upon waking, assume a vertical posture without hesitation or negotiation. Refrain from using your phone until you have engaged in an activity that benefits you personally, not work-related or for others. Engage in a physical action, such as making the bed, stepping outside, or drinking water, that signals to your body that you are awake and ready to begin. Make a decision and select the one task you intend to accomplish that propels you forward.

Motivation is not necessary; instead, focus on movement. Clarity is not required; a starting point is sufficient.

The initial 10 minutes serve as the pivotal moment.

The Mechanism of Effectiveness

By sending a signal to your brain, you assert control over your actions, not fear, distractions, or external influences.

Confidence is not acquired through thought alone; it is cultivated through behaviour. This transformation commences when you cease reacting and embrace movement.

Those initial 10 minutes are not about completing every task; rather, they are about establishing a sense of authority.

Adopting an assertive posture aligns with your brain's response, fostering a more effective approach.

Conclusion

To enhance your confidence, clarity, power, and momentum, it is crucial to seize control of the initial 10 minutes of your day.

Achieving this may not be flawless or accompanied by fanfare; rather, it requires intentional effort.

By taking ownership of your time and energy from the outset, you cease to wait for a state of readiness and actively prepare for success.

This, my friend, is the foundation upon which individuals construct their days—one decision, one action, and one resolute 10-minute block at a time.

Tools to Cultivate Self-Trust Through Consistent Self-Complying

Contrary to popular belief, confidence cannot be faked, nor can it be achieved through mental reasoning or delayed gratification.

However, self-trust serves as the bedrock upon which confidence is built. Without self-trust, confidence is akin to a house constructed on sand, susceptible to collapse upon encountering setbacks.

Let us acknowledge the frequency with which we make promises to ourselves but fail to follow through. Common examples include:

- "I will commence my tasks tomorrow."
- "I will engage in physical exercise after work."
- "I will take a risk once I feel prepared."

These unfulfilled promises can lead to feelings of failure and erode self-trust. When self-trust is diminished, confidence becomes an elusive ideal.

Nevertheless, there is hope. I am about to demonstrate a simple yet effective method for rebuilding self-trust.

1. Establishing Small-Scale Trust: Building Trust One Tiny Promise at a Time

It is essential to clarify that self-trust is not an instantaneous achievement nor can it be attained by setting grandiose and unrealistic goals.

Instead, it is cultivated through the gradual accumulation of small, achievable promises.

For instance, if you are prone to setting ambitious goals such as "I will lose 50 pounds" or "I will compose a book," but subsequently abandon them when life presents challenges, you are inadvertently deepening your self-doubt.

Therefore, it is advisable to adopt a more incremental approach.

Set forth a promise that is so simple and straightforward that there is no compelling reason to neglect it.

Consider the following examples:

- "I will consume one glass of water upon waking."
- "I will make my bed immediately after waking."
"Today, I intend to engage in a five-minute walk."

This objective appears straightforward, yet its significance lies in its simplicity. Maintain a manageable scope and ensure its feasibility. Each instance of fulfilling a small commitment fosters self-trust. By acknowledging your commitment and its execution, you establish a solid foundation for achieving more ambitious goals.

Sounds simple, right? That's the point. Keep it small, and keep it doable. Because each time you keep a small promise, you build trust with yourself. You tell your brain: "I said I would do this. And I did it." That's how you lay the foundation for the bigger goals you want to crush.

2. Set Achievable Goals: Avoid Overwhelming Ambitions

While it is admirable to have ambitious goals, it is crucial to set specific and achievable objectives. Setting vague goals, such as "I want to be successful" or "I want to be fit," can lead to disappointment and hinder progress.

To achieve success, it is essential to establish specific, achievable, and manageable goals. For instance, instead of saying "I want to be healthier," you could set a goal to walk for 10 minutes every morning. Similarly, instead of "I want to be more organised," you could set a goal to organise one drawer in your kitchen each day. And instead of "I want to be more productive," you could set a goal to write one paragraph each morning.

By making your goals clear and achievable, you will build momentum and self-trust, which are essential for achieving your objectives.

3. Implement the Countdown practice to Honour Your Promises

The Countdown practice is a powerful tool that can help you honour your promises to yourself. It is not just a method for avoiding procrastination; it is also a way to maintain your commitment to your goals.

When you make a promise to yourself, whether it is a small task like drinking a glass of water or a larger task like sending an email, it is important to take action immediately. Do not wait for motivation or a perfect moment to start.

Here is how you can implement the Countdown practice:

* **Identify the Promise:** When you make a promise to yourself, take note of it.
* **Count Down:** Begin counting down from 5 to 1.
* **Take Action:** As you count down, take action towards your promise. Move forward and start working on the task.

The moment you hesitate or doubt yourself, your brain will likely find excuses to delay the task. By implementing the Countdown practice, you can overcome these obstacles and take action on your promises. Regularly practicing this technique can lead to a significant improvement in your self-trust and self-reliance.

4. Hold Yourself Accountable: The Only Path to Success

The realisation that you are the sole individual responsible for fulfilling your commitments can be disheartening. It is crucial to acknowledge that relying on external sources for permission to succeed is an unrealistic expectation. Self-trust is built upon the consistent fulfilment of one's own promises, and this principle serves as the foundation for genuine confidence.

5. Reframe Setbacks: Embrace Learning and Perseverance

The true test of self-trust lies in the inevitable occurrence of setbacks. It is essential to refrain from succumbing to despair when faced with failures. Instead of allowing a broken promise to define one's worth or capabilities, reframe it as an opportunity for growth and learning.

Reflect on the fact that everyone experiences setbacks. However, these moments do not define an individual unless they allow them to overshadow their progress. They are merely stepping stones in the journey of self-improvement. When you encounter a setback in fulfilling a promise, take a moment to reflect on the circumstances and identify areas for improvement. Ask yourself:

- What led to the failure?
- What actions can I take to avoid similar mistakes in the future?

By acknowledging these challenges and taking proactive steps to rectify them, you can regain your momentum and continue your journey of self-trust.

Conclusion:

To cultivate confidence, it is essential to begin by fostering self-trust. The most effective method to achieve this is by consistently fulfilling your self-imposed commitments.

Begin by setting achievable, manageable objectives. Implement the Countdown practice to maintain focus and accountability. Refrain from giving up when you encounter setbacks.

Trust is not established through grandiose gestures; rather, it is cultivated through consistent, small actions that demonstrate your reliability.

By adopting these strategies, you can develop a robust and enduring sense of confidence.

PART 3

LIVING LOUD

In this section, you will discover the transformative power of confidence. You have acquired the knowledge of its construction and the ability to rewire your brain for its development. Now, it is time to embody this confidence. No longer will you retreat into silence, await invitations, or shrink, apologise, or seek permission to assert yourself.

Here, you will learn how to stand tall, speak assertively, and present yourself as the authentic individual you were destined to be before the world instilled in you a sense of caution.

How to Speak Up, Even When You're Scared

Allow me to convey a message that I wish someone had shared with me at the age of 19, 29, or even yesterday: Your voice holds significance—even if it trembles during your initial attempt to express yourself.

If you have ever reflected on a conversation and felt a sense of regret for not speaking up, or if you have ever remained silent in a meeting while someone less qualified assumed control, I empathise with you. If you have ever suppressed your genuine opinions to maintain harmony, you are not alone in this experience.

However, it is essential to acknowledge that confidence does not manifest in an ostentatious manner. It is not flawless or granted without permission.

Confidence involves speaking up when every part of your body yearns to retreat. It entails asserting your thoughts, even if your voice wavers.

How to Communicate Your Truth in a World That Favours Noise

Let us address the crux of the matter: we reside in a society where the individual who raises their voice most frequently often gains the opportunity to speak. Social media platforms tend to favour extreme expressions, and meetings often reward the confident individual who presents themselves with nothing novel to share but conveys their ideas with conviction. In contrast, the intelligent and thoughtful individuals are often compelled to suppress their opinions, waiting patiently, planning meticulously, and refining their perspectives.

Here's the issue: if you persist in waiting to be "ready," you will continue to observe less qualified individuals taking your position.

Confidence is not about being the most intelligent, articulate, or polished. It is about being willing to express your thoughts, even if your voice trembles.

Realistically, speaking your truth is not always glamorous or fashionable. In fact, it is often awkward, intimidating, and even causes physical discomfort.

However, this is genuine confidence—the kind that is not performative but powerful. It is not about generating noise; it is about demonstrating courage.

Your truth is significant, even if it makes others uncomfortable. Even if no one applauds. Even if someone raises an eyebrow. Even if they misinterpret your intentions.

Because speaking your truth is not about altering the world's perspective. It is about transforming your own.

Each time you use your voice, even in small, everyday interactions, you are reminding yourself: I am important. My thoughts are important. My perspective is valuable.

Therefore, how do you begin?

Cease Seeking the Ideal Moment

Abandon your quest for the perfect moment. Refrain from editing yourself mid-sentence. Disregard the desire for approval and focus on honesty.

Practice Self-Compassion:

The next time you perceive a diminution in your ideas, needs, or emotions, pause. Take a deep breath and count from five to one.

Speak Your Truth

Even if your speech is imperfect, unpolished, or creates a moment of silence.

Your presence is not meant to be background noise. Your purpose is to articulate yourself clearly, bravely, and unreservedly.

Remember, Your Voice Matters

Your voice does not require shouting to be heard.

The key is to silence your inner voice and speak your truth.

Scripts for Difficult Conversations

Addressing challenging conversations is a common apprehension. These conversations often evoke discomfort and anxiety. You may find yourself rehearsing negative scenarios or dismissing their significance.

However, the underlying truth is that you avoid confronting issues due to the fear of discomfort.

It is understandable that difficult conversations can be daunting, whether with a superior, partner, parents, best friend, or even yourself. They may feel like confronting a formidable obstacle. Nevertheless, it is crucial to recognise that:

Avoiding difficult conversations leads to more challenging lives.

Do you avoid discussing a raise with your boss? You remain underpaid. Do you avoid discussing a bothersome issue with your partner? You build silent resentment. Do you avoid setting boundaries with your friend? You start avoiding the friendship.

Difficult conversations do not break relationships; they reveal their strength.

And here's the key: you do not need perfect words. You simply need to start.

So let us cease overthinking and begin practicing. Below are some practical and effective scripts that you can rely on—so the next time your heart races and your mind screams "Don't say it!", you will have something stronger: your truth.

1. At Work: Requesting Your Deserved Compensation

You have been diligently working, taking on additional responsibilities, and contributing to the team's success. However, your title, compensation, or recognition have not kept pace with your efforts. This situation can be frustrating. Instead of suppressing your concerns, you may find yourself dismissing them as "fine."

However, it is crucial to acknowledge that this is not an acceptable state of affairs. Here is a suggested approach:

"Over the past six months, I have assumed greater responsibilities within my role and have consistently delivered results that I am proud of. I would like to schedule a meeting to discuss my compensation and explore opportunities for professional growth. I value this position and am eager to advance within the company."

This approach is straightforward, clear, and professional. It establishes a respectful dialogue that allows you to express your needs and aspirations.

If this approach makes you feel uncomfortable, it is a positive sign that your concerns are valid. Do not hesitate to address them.

2. In Relationships: Expressing Concerns Openly

In relationships, it is crucial to communicate openly and honestly about any concerns or issues that may be affecting the dynamics of the partnership.

Example Script:

"I would like to discuss a matter that has been on my mind. I have been hesitant to bring it up because I do not wish to create tension, but I believe that honesty is essential for the health of our relationship."

This approach demonstrates vulnerability and invites the conversation without resorting to blame or criticism. Instead, you are taking responsibility for your feelings and how they impact the relationship.

Continuing the Conversation:

"When you engage in [specific behaviour], I experience [your emotion]. I do not intend to assign blame, but rather to express my feelings honestly because they influence my behaviour and interactions within the relationship."

The format "When you ___, I feel ___" is particularly effective in conveying emotional intelligence. It allows you to articulate your feelings without resorting to excessive emotional expression or lengthy monologues.

3. Establishing Boundaries with Friends: A Balancing Act

Even with the closest of friends, it is essential to establish boundaries without causing guilt or tension.

Consider a scenario where a friend consistently cancels plans at the last minute, makes jokes at your expense, or disregards your personal boundaries.

Instead of abruptly ending the friendship or pretending everything is acceptable, try the following approach:

"I value our friendship deeply, but I have something important to discuss. I have been hesitant to bring it up because I did not want to create conflict, but it is crucial for our mutual well-being."

Observe the pattern: approach the conversation with sensitivity and honesty.

“Recently, I have observed that when you engage in [specific behaviour], it affects me negatively. I feel [emotion]. I am sharing this because I care about our relationship.”

Many individuals are unaware of the impact of their actions until they are directly confronted. Your silence inadvertently normalises their behaviour, while your honesty empowers them to develop a deeper appreciation for your friendship.

4. Self-Reflection: The Most Vital Conversation of Your Life

Occasionally, the most challenging conversation is not with another individual—it is with oneself.

Consider the following scenarios:

* The dream you have been postponing.
* The accurate information regarding your health, finances, and habits.
* The toxic relationship from which you are too apprehensive to depart.

Begin by acknowledging your discomfort and expressing your readiness to confront the truth:

“I cannot continue to deny the impact of this matter. I am prepared to cease evading the truth.”

Subsequently, pose the following questions:

* What are my genuine desires?
* What actions would I take if I were not burdened by fear?

Speak these truths aloud, write them down, or even look yourself in the mirror if necessary. However, cease deceiving yourself. You are entitled to the truth.

The Significance of Effective Scripts in Confrontational Situations

Contrary to popular belief, complex conversations do not necessitate elaborate speeches. Instead, they require:

* **Honesty:** Transparency and forthrightness in communication.
* **Clarity:** Precision and specificity in expressing your thoughts and feelings.
* **Courage:** Embracing challenges and overcoming obstacles in difficult situations.

By adopting a vulnerable approach rather than attributing blame, you disarm the other party and foster a more receptive atmosphere. Utilising specific examples instead of generalisations ensures that your message remains grounded in truth. Furthermore, beginning by expressing your emotions rather than focusing solely on their actions empowers you to maintain control of the conversation.

It is important to acknowledge that initially employing these scripts may evoke discomfort and anxiety. Overthinking and self-doubt are common responses. However, it is crucial to remember that confronting discomfort is a necessary step for personal growth and development. Thriving solely in avoidance hinders personal progress and prevents individuals from confronting their challenges effectively.

Enhancing Communication: Countdown practice for Confrontational Discussions

When faced with the prospect of engaging in a challenging conversation, it is common to experience a sense of apprehension. However, there is a simple yet effective strategy to overcome this fear and initiate a productive dialogue: employ Countdown practice.

Countdown practice:

1. **Begin Counting:** Start by silently counting down from five to one.
2. **Speak the First Sentence:** Once the countdown reaches one, speak the first sentence of your conversation.

By employing this technique, you can effectively interrupt your internal fear and begin the conversation.

The Importance of Confrontation:

Confrontational discussions are crucial for personal growth and development. They are not mere detours; rather, they serve as the primary pathways to self-improvement. The more you practice confronting difficult issues, the less daunting they will become.

Your purpose in engaging in these conversations is not to maintain peace at the expense of your truth. Rather, your goal is to establish genuine relationships, establish clear boundaries, and build a fulfilling life rooted in honesty and integrity.

Consequently, it is imperative to express oneself, even if the conversation is intricate, contentious, or emotionally taxing. Embrace your vulnerability and permit your voice to resonate with authenticity.

For your truth is not excessive. It has simply been awaiting your articulation.

How to Overcome Judgment, Rejection, and Awkward Silence

Frankly, one of the primary reasons individuals refrain from speaking up, pursuing their desires, or taking significant, audacious actions is the apprehension of others' perceptions.

This apprehension is indeed tangible, profound, and human. It is deeply ingrained in your brain, akin to a smoke alarm, triggering an immediate response whenever you contemplate engaging in any activity that may result in judgment, rejection, or silence.

Your brain's internal dialogue may manifest as follows:

"What if they mock me?"

"What if I make an error?"

"What if I appear foolish?"

"What if no one responds?"

It is crucial to comprehend the following:

Judgment, rejection, and silence are not the end of the world. They are the price of admission for a life you are proud of.

Let us examine each of these concepts in detail. You will discover that none of them are as potent—or perilous—as you initially perceived.

1. Judgment: It is About Them, Not You

To begin, let us clarify that individuals are prone to judging various aspects of life, including one's attire, speech, silence, occupation, willingness to express oneself, willingness to pursue new endeavours, and adherence to established norms.

Achieving their approval is an unattainable goal, as the standards are continually evolving.

Furthermore, it is crucial to recognise that judgment is not a reflection of your inherent worth; rather, it serves as a projection of their own perspectives and biases.

Consider this: when someone judges you, they are essentially projecting their own insecurities, fears, beliefs, and preconceived notions onto you. The focus is not on you; it is on their own experiences and perspectives.

Therefore, it is imperative that we refrain from entrusting our self-worth to individuals who are merely transient in our lives and lack any genuine stake in our well-being.

The reality is that you will inevitably be judged regardless of your actions. Consequently, it may be more advantageous to be judged while engaging in activities that align with your beliefs and values.

2. Rejection: The Data That Embraces Freedom

Rejection may evoke a sense of failure, but it is not inherently negative. Rather, it serves as valuable information, feedback, and a redirection of your efforts.

Consider scenarios such as pitching an idea to your supervisor and receiving a negative response, asking someone out and not receiving interest, or launching a project without garnering substantial support. While these experiences can be emotionally challenging, they provide valuable insights and demonstrate your persistence and willingness to take risks. It is crucial to recognise that rejection does not imply a lack of competence or worth. Rather, it signifies your courage in seeking greater opportunities and stepping outside your comfort zone. By embracing rejection as a stepping stone, you cultivate self-belief and resilience.

Individuals who consistently avoid rejection may be missing out on valuable experiences and opportunities for growth. Remember, your worth is not defined by your successes or failures. Instead, focus on your progress and celebrate your achievements, no matter how small they may seem.

Rejection: A Filter, Not a Final Decision

Rejection serves as a filter, not a definitive conclusion. It eliminates incompatible options, enabling you to discern what aligns with your goals. The next time you encounter a negative response, express gratitude and continue your pursuit.

Awkward Silence: A Common Brain Reaction

Imagine this scenario: you contribute to a meeting, but no one responds. You express your feelings, but they remain silent. You pose a vulnerable question, and the room falls into a state of silence.

Welcome to the recurring nightmare your brain creates: awkward silence.

However, it is crucial to understand that awkward silence does not imply a personal failure.

Silence can signify that individuals are engaged in processing information. It may indicate discomfort, which is beyond your responsibility to alleviate. Alternatively, it could be a manifestation of your courage, as the room struggles to comprehend your response.

In some instances, silence is simply silence.

Refrain from filling it, rushing to apologise, or succumbing to self-doubt due to a lack of applause.

True confidence lies in the ability to maintain composure during pauses without succumbing to panic.

Express your thoughts, take a deep breath, stay grounded, and allow the pause to exist with authority.

Validation is not a prerequisite for recognising the significance of your voice. You are already cognizant of its importance.

Let us now consider practical strategies to navigate challenging situations in real life:

1. **Reframe the Threat:** Your mind perceives judgment and rejection as existential threats. However, you are not a primitive individual being expelled from a community. You are an adult with the ability to make decisions. Reframe your thoughts by acknowledging that:

"I am not in imminent danger. I am merely experiencing discomfort."

2. **Implement the Countdown practice:** When your mind attempts to spiral into a negative thought pattern, interrupt the cycle. Employ the Countdown practice:

- **5:** Identify a specific object or item.
- **4:** Recall a memory of a positive experience.
- **3:** Name a physical sensation you are experiencing.
- **2:** Name a familiar person.
- **1:** Breathe deeply and stand your ground. Refrain from retreating or retreating from the situation.

3. **Prepare for the Worst-Case Scenario:** Consider the potential consequences of the situation and identify the most extreme outcome.

Spoiler Alert: The most likely outcome is discomfort, not catastrophe. You can endure someone's lack of appreciation, the absence of a response, or awkwardness.

4. **Establish a Reminder Phrase:** Prior to a significant event, repeat to yourself:

"I have overcome more challenging obstacles than this."

Alternatively, you can affirm:

"Perfection is not a prerequisite. Authenticity is sufficient."

5. Celebrate Your Courage—Not Just Your Outcomes

Each time you speak up, try, risk, ask, or show up, you are developing emotional resilience. You are taking action that most people avoid throughout their lives. This deserves recognition and celebration.

Final Truth

To build genuine confidence, you must cease allowing fear of judgment or rejection to dictate your decisions.

For the life you desire,

The Path to Desired Outcomes

The relationship you desire, the career you aspire to, and the impact you wish to make—all lie beyond the daunting, awkward, and overwhelming moments.

While it is possible that you may encounter judgment, rejection, or silence, it is crucial to remember that you will persist in your pursuit of your goals.

Building Confidence in Relationships, Parenting, and Leadership

Let us commence with a truth that many individuals are hesitant to acknowledge:

The absence of self-confidence significantly influences the dynamics of all relationships, both personal and professional.

Self-doubt manifests in various ways, including overthinking every interaction, apologising for trivial matters, and questioning parenting, leadership, and self-worth.

This pervasive low-grade self-doubt manifests in subtle yet significant ways.

For instance, it manifests in hesitation before setting boundaries, shrinking in meetings, and snapping at children not because they are out of line, but due to underlying concerns about their own inadequacy as parents.

The Importance of Confidence in Relationships, Parenting, and Leadership

In each of these roles, you occupy a pivotal position, setting the tone and establishing the desired atmosphere. Consequently, cultivating confidence is not merely beneficial; it is essential for achieving your objectives.

Furthermore, when you lead with confidence—not arrogance, not control, but grounded self-trust—everything transforms.

1. Building Confidence in Relationships: Embracing Authenticity

In the realm of relationships, confidence should not be misconstrued as dominance or the pursuit of absolute knowledge. True confidence lies in self-assurance and self-acceptance, enabling individuals to maintain their individuality while fostering meaningful connections with others.

Regrettably, many individuals succumb to the pressure of people-pleasing, suppressing their true selves and diminishing their personalities. This tendency to suppress desires in order to maintain harmony can lead to a lack of genuine peace and fulfilment.

Authentic peace emerges from clarity, courage, and effective communication. When individuals cultivate confidence, they cease to question their actions and instead assert their needs and desires with assertiveness. For instance, instead of asking, "Is it okay if I bring this up?", they might say, "This matters to me, so I am bringing it up."

When you possess self-assurance, you refrain from pursuing individuals who exhibit inconsistent behaviour. You do not tolerate hot-and-cold treatment. You no longer feel compelled to constantly demonstrate your lovability, as you are fully aware of your worth.

Confidence empowers you to receive love rather than constantly performing for it. It facilitates effective communication of your needs without the need for apology. It instills the strength to depart from a relationship when it demands self-sacrifice.

It is crucial to acknowledge that the ideal relationship will never necessitate the diminution of your authentic self.

2. Confidence in Parenting: You Are Not Failing as Profoundly as You Perceive

Parenting can be an arduous journey, leading to a constant sense of inadequacy.

Parents may find themselves resorting to yelling when they intended to maintain composure, succumbing to demands when they should have stood firm, or questioning the cause of their child's tantrum, attributing it to a seemingly insignificant oversight, such as providing peanut butter twice last week instead of almond butter.

It is essential to recognise that there is no such thing as a perfect parent. However, a confident parent possesses a transformative impact.

Confident parents, despite their imperfections, demonstrate a presence and willingness to acknowledge their mistakes.

Parents do not need to control every outcome; instead, they guide, adjust, and trust their abilities along the way.

Confidence in parenting manifests in the following statements:

“Although I may not possess all the answers, I trust my judgment to discern the appropriate course of action.”

“I am not compelled to adhere to every parenting trend available on the internet. I am intimately acquainted with my child’s unique needs and characteristics.”

“Even when I make mistakes, my presence and commitment are more important than perfection.”

Furthermore, confident parents foster confident children through the power of modelling rather than lecturing.

When children witness their parents assert themselves, attempt to overcome challenges, persist in their efforts, apologise without embarrassment, and demonstrate laughter, love, and leadership without the need for perfection, they gain permission to embrace their authentic selves.

3. Confidence in Leadership: Trust Yourself Assertively

Whether leading a team, classroom, business, or family, leadership is predicated on energy.

This energy emanates from confidence.

A confident leader does not require being the most intelligent individual in the room. They do not necessitate possessing all the answers. They do not lead by fear; instead, they lead by clarity.

Confident leadership manifests in the following ways:

* **Active Listening:** They prioritise listening over speaking, not out of fear of others' ideas.
* **Credit Recognition:** They acknowledge and appreciate others' contributions, not driven by insecurity about their own value.
* **Decision-Making:** They take action, even when the path is uncertain, trusting their ability to adjust course.

Confident leadership is not driven by ego; it is a harmonious blend of humility and bold action.

It involves standing up when something feels amiss, inviting others to participate rather than criticising them. It entails embodying the kind of leadership that one would have desired.

Admittedly, there will be judgment, occasional mistakes, and challenging conversations. However, confident leaders do not wait for a perfect moment; they take action regardless.

Here is a crucial revelation:

Confidence is not acquired first; it is cultivated through leadership. By leading, confidence naturally develops.

Tactical Leadership: Building Confidence in All Aspects of Life

1. Embrace Connection, Not Perfection: In relationships, parenting, and leadership, individuals seek genuine connections rather than perfection.

2. Self-Reflection: Prioritise Clarity Over Fear: Before engaging in conversations, making decisions, or taking actions, question whether you are acting from fear or clarity.

3. Cultivate Self-Trust: Confidence does not equate to invulnerability; it lies in the belief in one's ability to recover from setbacks.

4. The Countdown practice: Confront your fears, count down, and take action regardless. Whether it involves initiating challenging conversations, establishing boundaries, or leading meetings, the decision to act from within is invaluable.

5. Consistent Self-Selection: Confidence involves repeatedly choosing oneself, even in daunting situations, when there is no applause, and when one's voice trembles.

Conclusion

Confidence in relationships, parenting, and leadership does not reside in being louder, more correct, or flawless. It stems from aligning one's actions with core values, relying on intuition, and acting with purpose. It's about showing up even when you're not sure how it'll land. It's about knowing that you exactly as you are are enough.
And when you lead with that kind of confidence?
By extending this permission to others, you inadvertently grant them the same freedom to act in the same manner.

How to Take Up Space in a World That Asks You to Shrink

There is a pattern you have been unconsciously adopting. When you enter a room, you sense the energy, and without conscious effort, you diminish your presence.

In meetings, you suppress your opinions, avoiding the opportunity to express yourself. You downplay your enthusiasm to prevent being perceived as overly enthusiastic. You minimise your accomplishments with friends who are still developing their careers.

You become a chameleon, conforming to others' expectations. A diminished version of yourself, because you have learned that it is perceived as safer to be small than to be authentic.

Let us acknowledge the truth: you are not being humble; you are concealing your true self.

This behaviour must cease.

Concealing your true self does not provide protection. It does not enhance the perception of others towards you. It does not foster trust, safety, or meaningful connections.

It merely erodes your sense of self-identity.

People-Pleasing, Approval Addiction, and Playing Small

Contrary to popular belief, most individuals are not born with a confidence deficit.
Individuals are conditioned to develop such a deficit.

From birth, you were loud, curious, and bold. Over time, you learned to be quiet, cautious, and accommodating.

This process commences early. Someone may instruct you:

"Be less vocal."
"Refrain from causing trouble."
"Be amiable."
"Cease displaying ostentation."

Gradually, you begin editing yourself, seeking approval as if it were a drug. You become addicted to being liked, even if it entails being disingenuous.

Allow me to illustrate how this manifests in adulthood:

- Agreeing when you intend to decline.
- Allowing your phone to ring out rather than disappointing someone.
- Reducing your accomplishments to avoid making others feel inferior.
- Withholding ideas due to your apprehension that they are inadequate.

However, approval is a shifting target.

Regardless of how diminutive you make yourself, someone will still criticise you. Undeterred by your efforts to project likability, someone will still misinterpret your intentions.

Consequently, if you are destined to be judged, it may be preferable to be judged while being authentic.

Why Dimming Your Light Does Not Benefit Anyone

You may perceive shrinking as a noble act, believing it makes you more approachable and contributes to maintaining peace.

However, this notion is misguided.

By diminishing your presence, you inadvertently convey the message that your needs are inconsequential and your voice should be disregarded. Your light should only illuminate when it aligns with the convenience of others.

It is crucial to understand that your light does not cause blindness; rather, it illuminates the possibilities for others.

When you assert yourself, speak up, and stand tall, you empower others to do the same.

The woman in the back of the meeting is observing your actions. The friend trapped in a toxic relationship witnesses your boundary setting. Your child learns bravery by observing your courageous approach.

Acceptance does not necessitate the diminution of your joy, nor does shrinking your success make others feel comfortable. You do not need to shrink simply because someone else has not yet reached their full potential.

Confidence is not about overpowering others; it is about standing in your own space without the need for apology.

Embracing Authenticity: Navigating Challenges and Building Self-Confidence

It is important to acknowledge that when you embrace your true self, not everyone will be receptive.

Some individuals may have preferred you when you were more accommodating, conforming to their expectations by consistently agreeing or sharing humour that may not have been universally appreciated. However, it is crucial to recognise that this is no longer your responsibility.

Here are some key points to remember:

- You are entitled to occupy your own space and express your opinions, even if they may be controversial.
- You are permitted to celebrate your achievements, regardless of whether others share in your enthusiasm.
- Your purpose is not to be easily assimilated; rather, it is to be authentic and genuine.

Being fully authentic entails the following:

- Declining requests without excessive explanation.
- Sharing your enthusiasm without apprehension about potential disapproval.

- Departing from environments that compel you to adopt a persona that is not aligned with your true self.

While embracing your authenticity may initially evoke discomfort, it will lead to the development of self-trust, which is the foundation of confidence.

“You Are Not Excessive—They Are Simply Not Adequate.”

Have you heard this phrase before?

“You are too intense.”
“You are too driven.”
“You are too emotional.”
“You are too ambitious.”

Let me be direct:

You are not excessive. You are simply surrounded by individuals who are insufficient for your purpose. If someone cannot comprehend your fullness, it is a reflection of their limitations—not yours. The next time someone labels you as “too much,” remind yourself of this:

“I am not excessive. I am finally being all of myself.”

You are not obligated to present a diminished version of yourself to the world. You are owed a life that resonates with authenticity.

Let’s Talk Tactics: How to Stop Shrinking

1. Self-Editing Awareness:

Identify instances when you suppress your opinions, compromise your authenticity, or hesitate to express yourself.

Reflect on the following question: "Am I being genuine, or am I prioritising social approval?"

2. Unapologetic Expression:

Begin with small actions, such as sharing a photograph, expressing a thought, or wearing an outfit that aligns with your preferences. Embrace your natural laughter.

The world values authenticity over polished perfection.

3. Assertive Negotiation:

Practice asserting your boundaries without providing a follow-up explanation.

"No" constitutes a complete sentence, and confident individuals employ it assertively.

4. Physical Presence:

Uncross your arms, uncurl your body, adopt a posture of belonging, and walk with purpose.

Your physical presence communicates your self-worth to your brain. Act in accordance with this belief.

5. Surround Yourself with Supportive Individuals:

Identify individuals who challenge you positively, celebrate your progress, and acknowledge your enthusiasm.

Final Word

You have spent an excessive amount of time being smaller than you are.

This was done to maintain peace, make others feel comfortable, and avoid judgment.

However, shrinking does not provide protection; it merely confines you.

This chapter serves as your permission slip:

You are permitted to occupy space, express your true self, cease apologising, and embrace a more assertive lifestyle.

Therefore, cease shrinking to conform.

You do not fit into a predefined mould; you were created to break free from it.

People-Pleasing, Approval Addiction, and Playing Small

Allow me to confront you with the stark reality:

If your sole objective is to ensure the happiness of others, you are not living your life; you are merely living theirs.

Here is a revised version of the provided text:

In this scenario, you exhibit an excessive agreeableness. You apologise when you are not genuinely sorry. You refrain from speaking up, as expressing your opinions is perceived as riskier than maintaining silence.

When you lack remorse, you refrain from speaking up, perceiving the risk of disrupting the status quo as greater than the discomfort of silence. You acquiesce even when every fibre of your being resists.

This behaviour exemplifies people-pleasing and approval addiction, which are significant hindrances for intelligent, capable, and talented individuals.

It is understandable that we have been conditioned to conform to these expectations since childhood.

Raise your hand if you have ever been instructed to:
"Be pleasant."
"Refrain from making a fuss."
"Avoid being difficult."
"Ensure everyone's comfort."

Such directives have a lasting impact.

Consequently, as adults, we often equate confidence with arrogance and confuse being liked with being respected. Every time we experience discomfort about disappointing someone, we experience a gradual diminution of our self-assurance.

Let us acknowledge this phenomenon as playing small.

Approval as a Drug

People-pleasing is addictive, and the drug you seek is approval.

Approval provides a temporary rush of validation, a sense of belonging, and a respite from the anxiety of standing out. However, like any drug, the high dissipates, leaving you at the starting point, awaiting the next individual's permission to feel good about yourself.

This state is not freedom; it is emotional dependence. You are outsourcing your self-worth.

A stark reality is that no amount of external approval will suffice until you approve of yourself.

The Cost of Playing Small

It is crucial to clarify that playing small is not a sign of humility; it is detrimental.

It entrenches individuals to anticipate lower expectations from you. It communicates to the world that you lack the confidence to express your voice effectively. It reinforces the notion that your presence is optional, when it is not.

Embracing Authenticity: Overcoming Self-Limiting Behaviours

Engaging in self-deprecating behaviour can hinder your growth in various aspects of life, including your career, relationships, and personal roles. It is essential to recognise that feeling overwhelmed is not necessarily indicative of inadequacy; rather, it suggests a lack of self-expression.

Suppressing your genuine thoughts, emotions, and boundaries can lead to resentment and hinder your personal development. It is crucial to acknowledge and address these suppressed aspects to prevent emotional distress and potential consequences.

Self-Reflection: Identifying Patterns of People-Pleasing

Take a moment to introspect and identify areas in your life where you prioritise the needs of others over your own. Consider the following questions:

- What are the unspoken truths that I am avoiding?
- Who am I trying to impress by suppressing my authentic self?
- What personal growth opportunities do I miss when I choose comfort over honesty?

Understanding these patterns is the foundation for personal transformation. Awareness empowers individuals to make conscious choices and break free from self-limiting behaviours.

How to Refrain from Shrinking

1. Identify and resist the urge to acquiesce solely for the sake of maintaining harmony. Pause and introspect: "Is this action in conflict with my principles, or driven by fear?"

2. Embrace discomfort. It is possible that declining a request may cause discomfort in others. This is acceptable, as you are not responsible for their emotional state.

3. Embrace the prospect of disappointing others. This may sound counterintuitive, but it is essential for personal growth. You will endure, and they will endure. Your self-respect will undoubtedly increase.

4. Celebrate your authenticity. Each time you communicate honestly, even if your voice trembles, acknowledge and appreciate this act. This is how you build confidence—immediately and through consistent action.

Conclusion

To live a purposeful and fulfilling life, it is crucial to abandon the notion that everyone will approve of your actions.

You are not an indispensable part of everyone's life. Your presence is not a prerequisite for their acceptance.

Your true essence—your vibrant, complex, and brilliant self—is what matters. Embrace your uniqueness and refuse to conform.

The individuals who are compatible with you will not require you to shrink; they will value your presence and authenticity.

The rest of the world can be disregarded. Your life is too precious to be lived in a muted manner.

Why Dimming Your Light Does Not Benefit Anyone

Pay attention, as this is of utmost importance:

When you reduce your presence to accommodate others, you deprive the world of the unique value that only you possess.

You have likely heard the adages: “Refrain from ostentation,” “Maintain humility,” and “Avoid excessive display.”

However, the truth they omit is that the world does not necessitate your diminution.

The world requires you to stand tall, to be present, and to embody your authentic self unreservedly. This necessitates a willingness to radiate—sometimes with brilliance, sometimes with prominence, and occasionally with greater intensity than others may be prepared for.

Therefore, it is crucial to clarify that dimming your light does not safeguard anyone; it merely hinders you from living the life you were destined for.

The Myth of Excessive Presence

It is common to believe that holding back serves others as a benevolent act. It appears as though you are creating space for individuals to flourish and shine. Perhaps you have been consistently advised to “moderate your behaviour,” “avoid excessive noise,” or “adopt a more reserved demeanour.”

Nevertheless, it is essential to recognise that this is merely their comfort zone speaking, not yours.

When you choose to shrink yourself, you are not demonstrating generosity; rather, you are sacrificing your true potential. You are playing small in a world that requires more individuals like you to step forward and take the lead.

There is no such thing as being too much. You are not too large, too bold, or too passionate. You are simply the right person, and anyone who is unable to handle your light is someone who is not meant to share your journey.

It is time for you to cease apologising for being yourself. The truth is, you have the right to exist in your full glory, regardless of whether those around you can handle it.

The Unspoken Cost of Playing Small

Every time you hold yourself back, every time you conceal your talents, opinions, and unique perspective, you are communicating to the universe that you are not enough.

You may not even be aware of it, but every time you choose to remain silent when you should speak up, every time you dilute your truth to avoid causing discomfort, you are internalising that message.

What is the consequence? You are depriving yourself of growth, genuine opportunities, and the profound satisfaction that arises from fulfilling your destiny.

Individuals seek leaders, visionaries, problem solvers, and creators. However, it is crucial to recognise that effective leadership, creativity, and problem-solving require active participation rather than passive waiting for permission.

Diminishing one's presence not only affects personal growth but also hinders the world's ability to benefit from one's unique talents and contributions.

Conversely, when individuals embrace their authentic selves and radiate their potential, they empower others to do the same. They become beacons of inspiration, guiding others towards self-expression and self-discovery.

Consider the impact of world leaders, innovators, and change-makers who chose to conceal their true selves. If they had believed in their limitations, the world would have been diminished in terms of vibrancy and progress.

By allowing oneself to shine, one creates a ripple effect that inspires others to do the same. This collective illumination fosters creativity, innovation, and profound human connections.

The purpose of one's existence is not to conform to average standards. Rather, it is to stand out and make a meaningful impact on the world.

Every time you hesitate to showcase your own brilliance, you are denying the world your most creative ideas and significant achievements.

You have been gifted with unique talents and experiences that are exclusively yours. You owe it to yourself and those around you to live boldly, be fully visible, assert your power and presence.

There is no need to apologise for your intelligence, success, or opinions. Refrain from conforming to others' comfort levels by playing down your abilities.

The truth is, the more you demonstrate your presence, the more others around you will rise to meet you at your level.

By ceasing to diminish your light, you are not merely transforming your life; you are also impacting the lives of those who come into contact with you.

Time to Cease Apologising for Your Brilliance

Therefore, here is the challenge: commence by embodying your most authentic self. Refrain from diminishing your brilliance. Speak up, stand tall, take up space, and radiate your full potential.

Should anyone advise you to reduce your intensity, respond with a smile and a nod, continuing your journey. Remember that your brilliance was never theirs to control.

The world eagerly anticipates your presence, showcasing your unapologetic brilliance.

Trust me, they will express their gratitude for it.

How to Be Fully Yourself, Even When It May Cause Discomfort to Others

Allow me to express this unequivocally:

Your purpose on this planet is not to ensure the comfort of others.

Your purpose is to be authentic, to express yourself boldly, fully, loudly, messily, awkwardly, and confidently.

However, I understand your approach. You have dedicated years to observing social cues, to sensing when you may be perceived as excessive—too passionate, too ambitious, too emotional, too loud, too intense. In response, you adopt a defensive strategy:

- You moderate your expression.
- You edit your behaviour.
- You minimise your presence.

Each time you employ these tactics, a part of your true self remains suppressed.

The True Reason Behind Your Cautious Approach

Let us confront the underlying issue: you are apprehensive about causing discomfort to others.

You have learned that displaying an overly assertive, intelligent, or self-assured demeanour may elicit negative reactions. Individuals may withdraw, criticise, or dismiss you. This perceived judgment, akin to rejection, prompts you to suppress your authentic self before it manifests.

The paradoxical nature of this situation lies in the fact that you are inadvertently rejecting yourself.

You have misconstrued safety for belonging. You believe that if you can maintain the happiness of others, you will be loved. However, the reality is that love and approval are not synonymous. One necessitates authenticity, while the other demands performance.

Consequently, you engage in performance. You adopt the version of yourself that appears most acceptable, the agreeable one, the one who avoids conflict, and the one who conforms.

Nevertheless, deep down, you acknowledge that your purpose is not to conform; your purpose is to stand out.

The Burden of Concealing Your True Self

Each time you suppress your opinions, minimise your accomplishments, or dismiss what genuinely matters to you solely to ensure the comfort of others, you are abandoning yourself.

This self-abandonment manifests in your confidence, energy, and aspirations. You may question why you feel disconnected, unmotivated, and uninspired. This is because your authentic self has not had a seat at the table of your own life for years.

The unequivocal truth is that you cannot live a fulfilling life if you are expending your energy trying to avoid the discomfort of others.

You were not created to blend in; you were created to shine— and occasionally, shining may involve causing discomfort to a few individuals. This is acceptable.

You are not responsible for their reaction; you are responsible for your truth.

What "Being Fully You" Actually Looks Like

Being fully you is not about being reckless or self-centred. It is not about dominating every room or speaking over others.

It is about alignment.

It is walking into a room and not feeling the need to transform into a version of yourself that conforms to others' expectations.

It is expressing your genuine thoughts, not those that are safe to say.

It is dressing in a manner that reflects your personal style, laughing genuinely, expressing emotions without apology, and not filtering every thought through the lens of whether it will make someone uncomfortable.

It is recognising that your presence is sufficient. That you do not need to earn space; you already belong.

You are not a burden. You are not "too much." You are the exact amount of you that was meant to be here.

Not Everyone Will Like You—And That's the Point

This aspect often perplexes individuals: certain individuals may feel uneasy about your authentic self, leading them to distance themselves, criticise, and label you.

Accept this.

For when you present yourself fully as your true self, those who are not compatible with you will naturally distance themselves, and that is how the right individuals find you.

You should not surround yourself with individuals who only appreciate a diluted version of yourself. This is not genuine connection; it is merely a performance.

Allow those who cannot handle your authentic self to self-select out of your life. This is not rejection; it is refinement.

Your purpose is not to be universally liked; your purpose is to be deeply known.

Practice Being Uncomfortable

To embody your true self fully, you must cultivate the ability to tolerate discomfort.

You will need to speak when your voice trembles.

You will need to continue speaking when someone gazes at you with disapproval.

You will need to stand tall when the room falls silent.

You will need to disagree, express your refusal, establish boundaries, share significant ideas, and assert yourself—even when your heart races.

Achieving genuine confidence is not an effortless journey, but it is the path to self-assurance.

With each successful attempt, you impart a transformative lesson to your nervous system:

You are not obligated to surrender your authenticity for safety.

Allow Them to Feel Uncomfortable. Your Focus Should Be on Your Own Journey.

Adopt this mantra:

“If their discomfort arises, it is their responsibility, not yours.”

You have dedicated sufficient time to self-editing. Politeness, palatability, and professionalism are not prerequisites for respect. Authenticity is the key.

The individuals destined to be with you will not only accept your complete self but also love it. They will place greater trust in you, follow you more readily, and establish deeper connections. Most importantly, you will develop self-reliance.

Therefore, take a deep breath and embrace your space.

This world does not require an abundance of polished individuals masquerading as “adequate.” It thrives on the presence of genuine humans who are bold, assertive, unruly, and brimming with life.

Your journey begins with you.

“You Are Not Excessive—They Are Simply Not Adequate”

Let us remove the label immediately.

"Excessive."

Overly emotional. Loud. Ambitious. Sensitive. Direct. Intense. Bold. Intelligent. Opinionated.

Excessively.

You have likely encountered this sentiment before, albeit not in those precise terms, but you have experienced it. The stinging sensation when someone labels you as "extra." The disapproving glance when you express your passion. The awkward pause following an honest statement, as the atmosphere abruptly shifts.

You are familiar with this moment.

It sows a seed, prompting self-reflection.

Did I overreact? Did I express myself excessively? Was I too candid?

Allow me to be unequivocal: No. You were not.

You were simply being yourself.

Their discomfort is not your concern.

Why You've Been Shrinking Yourself

Upon emerging from the womb, you did not question your inherent worth. This notion was gradually instilled in you, piece by piece.

It manifested when someone instructed you to cease crying.

When they dismissed your aspirations with disdain.

When you were ridiculed for being “dramatic.”

When your instructor declared, “Allow someone else to provide an answer this time.”

When someone asserted, “Men are not attracted to women who speak excessively.”

Suddenly, you diminished your presence and subdued your brilliance. You made yourself more palatable.

Consequently, you adapted. You lowered your voice. You projected an aura of composure. You sought to receive less. You endeavoured to appear “calm.” You circumspectly navigated your own inherent power.

All in an effort to ensure that no one felt intimidated by the radiance of your being.

Allow me to convey a profound truth: you were never “too much.” They were merely insufficient to comprehend the value you possess.

The True Issue Lies Not with You, But with Them

When individuals express that you are “too much,” it is essential to understand the underlying reasons behind their perception.

Firstly, your presence may evoke discomfort because it reminds them of their own unfulfilled aspirations.

Secondly, you challenge their settled positions, prompting them to reconsider their established beliefs.

Thirdly, your actions reflect the freedom they yearn for but have suppressed within themselves.

Fourthly, your assertiveness may mirror the suppressed emotions and thoughts they have internalised.

It is crucial to recognise that these reactions are not a reflection of your inherent qualities, but rather a manifestation of their own unresolved issues.

Regrettably, you have taken on the responsibility of conforming to their expectations, thereby diminishing your own authenticity.

However, it is important to consider that if someone perceives you as being too assertive, it may be a reflection of their own introverted nature. Similarly, if they perceive you as ambitious, it could indicate that they have abandoned their own aspirations. If they perceive you as emotionally expressive, it might suggest a lack of emotional sensitivity on their part.

Therefore, it is imperative that you cease apologising for living a fully authentic life.

"Too Much" is a Disguised Compliment

Reframe this immediately: "Too much" is a coded expression of:

“I am unable to fully comprehend the entirety of your true self.”

Allow them to depart. When you compromise your authenticity to be accepted, you diminish the individuals who would have celebrated you at your full potential.

Your purpose is not to moderate; your objective is to amplify.

You are not intense; you are passionate. You are not aggressive; you are assertive. You are not dramatic; you are expressive. You are not bossy; you are a leader. You are not too much; you are more than sufficient.

And those who fail to perceive this?

They are not your companions.

Cease Seeking Approval from the Incorrect Audience

It is imperative to acknowledge that the majority of individuals who make you feel inadequate have not earned a privileged position in your life.

Therefore, why are you eagerly awaiting their permission?

Why are you diminishing your ideas, your voice, and your unique personality in pursuit of validation from someone who could not even comprehend a mere fraction of your true self?

You were not destined to be assimilated or conformed to. You were born to be undeniable and authentic.

The individuals who truly matter will comprehend your essence. They will embrace your authenticity and express their admiration for your genuine nature.

As for the rest, allow them to experience discomfort, make erroneous judgments, engage in gossip, abruptly end communication, and misunderstand your intentions.

It is not your responsibility to shrink yourself so that others may remain unchanged.

Embrace Your Authenticity

Here's your challenge: cease to be apprehensive when you excel.

Begin asserting yourself as if you were destined to do so. Speak more assertively. Laugh more heartily. Aspire to greater heights. Express your emotions with passion. Embrace your fervour. Speak the words that evoke fear within you. Present yourself with all your unique, brilliant, and audacious energy.

Take ownership of your narrative, your concepts, and your unwavering determination.

For when you embrace your "excessiveness," you grant others the permission to do the same.

And do not be surprised when individuals begin whispering, "Wow… I wish I possessed such bravery."

You are not excessively loud, overly sensitive, excessively opinionated, or excessively bold.

You are simply finally choosing to extinguish the dim light.

And we are grateful for this.

How to Give Yourself the Permission You've Been Waiting For

Allow me to pose a question to you, and I implore you to be candid with yourself.

What are you hesitating about?

Frankly, what are you waiting for to commence that business venture, submit your application for employment, express your opinions in that meeting, compose the book, relocate to the city, initiate the podcast, convey your true feelings, resign from the job you detest, or finally seize your opportunity?

For someone to suggest that you take action?

To gain additional experience?

To cultivate greater confidence?

To finally attain a state of readincss?

Allow me to deliver a blunt revelation that you may not have sought but desperately require:

No one is forthcoming to grant you permission.

Not your superior. Not your partner. Not your parents. Not your friends. Not the cosmos.

It is rightfully yours.

You are merely apprehensive about taking the plunge.

Here is a pattern I have repeatedly observed with intelligent, capable, and talented individuals—you may even recognise yourself in this.

You anticipate being selected.

You think, “If I merely exert myself diligently, someone will acknowledge my efforts.”

“If I demonstrate my worth, someone will provide me with an opportunity.”

“If I possess sufficient competence, someone will open the door for me.”

Allow me to emphatically assert that ceasing to wait for selection is imperative.

We were raised in systems that instilled the notion of waiting our turn. Raise your hand. Wait to be called upon. Wait to be promoted. Wait to be invited.

Such an approach is ineffective in real life.

Success does not originate from being chosen; it stems from self-selection.

Reflect upon every individual you admire—did they await permission? Certainly not.

They perceived an opportunity and, when it was secured, they seized it. They did not wait to be picked—they chose themselves.

And if you are idly waiting for a green light, here it is: ACT.

Unlocking Opportunities: A Proactive Approach

Opportunity is not a random occurrence; it is not a gift bestowed upon the fortunate few. Rather, it emerges when we take proactive steps and actively seek it out.

Societal norms often encourage us to remain passive, waiting for clarity, perfection, and a sense of safety before taking action. However, this approach is counterproductive.

The individuals who achieve success are those who embrace imperfection, take decisive leaps, and initiate their endeavours even before they feel fully prepared.

To cultivate opportunities, it is essential to break free from passive waiting and actively pursue them. This involves:

- **Proactive Communication:** Send emails, make calls, and engage in conversations without hesitation.
- **Embracing Action:** Take consistent action, even if it feels challenging or uncertain.
- **Building Confidence:** Confidence is not a fleeting emotion; it is the result of consistent effort and positive experiences.

Remember, confidence is not a passive state; it is a consequence of taking action and achieving success. By consistently pursuing opportunities and maintaining a proactive mindset, you can unlock your full potential and achieve your goals.

Embracing Ambition: Overcoming Fear and Achieving Your Goals

Allow me to share a transformative revelation that has profoundly impacted my life: fear should not be a deterrent; rather, it should be a catalyst for action.

Fear serves as an indication that you have reached the precipice of your comfort zone, beckoning you to venture beyond its boundaries.

While the majority of individuals succumb to fear and retreat, those who attain their aspirations embrace it with determination.

The apprehension surrounding failure, embarrassment, social judgments, and self-criticism serves as a precise compass, guiding you towards your true aspirations.

Jessica, the woman we encountered in Chapter 1, experienced an overwhelming sense of trepidation when she decided to speak up. Nevertheless, she persevered and took action.

Despite lacking confidence, she felt sufficiently prepared to act.

The key to success lies not in the absence of fear but in the courage to confront it, even for fleeting moments.

Bravery is not the absence of fear; it is the ability to act in defiance of it.

Therefore, pursue your aspirations with unwavering resolve, acknowledging the accompanying sensations of trepidation, discomfort, anxiety, and uncertainty. Ultimately, take the necessary action and send your message.

From Stuck to Self-Started

Here is the most liberating truth I can impart upon you:

You do not necessitate credentials, titles, platforms, or external validation to commence your journey.

The sole prerequisite is the commencement of action.

Confidence is not bestowed upon you; it is cultivated through consistent effort. Power is not bestowed upon you; it is acquired through determination.

You do not require permission to express yourself, assert your presence, articulate your truth, and transform your life.

You possess inherent worth, capability, and sufficiency.

The distinction between an individual who takes action and one who remains passive lies solely in the former's decision to move forward.

This chapter serves not merely as a motivational exhortation but also as a demarcation point.

You may choose to persist in waiting, harbouring hopes and devising strategies, or you may seize the opportunity to propel your life in the direction of your aspirations.

You do not require external validation or clarity; you must make a resolute decision and take decisive action.

Act now, for no one else will undertake the journey for you.

Deep within your subconscious, you have always been aware of this fundamental truth.

Killing the Desire to Be Chosen

Allow me to present a stark reality that many individuals spend their lives attempting to evade:

You are not ensnared; you are merely in a state of anticipation.

You await permission, validation, and recognition from others.

However, it is crucial to recognise that the "someone" you are waiting for will not materialise.

You have been conditioned to believe that success, opportunities, and recognition are bestowed upon you by external entities. You envision that individuals with authority or influence will acknowledge your worth, believe in your abilities, and ultimately grant you permission to take action.

This mindset manifests in various aspects of life. In educational settings, you eagerly await being called upon during class discussions. In athletic endeavours, the coach selects the starting players. In professional settings, promotions are bestowed upon individuals by their superiors. Even in personal matters, you assume that someone else will select you for significant life events such as love, success, leadership, and visibility.

Nevertheless, it is imperative to clarify that you do not require external validation; you are responsible for choosing yourself.

Before dismissing this notion as mere motivational rhetoric, allow me to elaborate on its significance.

The Unseen Obstacle: The Trap You May Not Recognise

Imagine this scenario:

You aspire to speak on stage, but you persistently await an invitation.
You yearn to lead, yet you patiently await someone to champion your cause.
You desire to launch your business, but you persistently wait for someone to endorse your concept.
You aspire to write, but you persistently wait for an offer to come your way.

Meanwhile, another individual—an individual with less talent, less experience, and less refinement—proceeds with their goals.

The reason behind this is that they did not wait for external validation; they took matters into their own hands.

The most poignant aspect of this situation is that you may have already been overlooked, not because you lacked the necessary qualities, but because you failed to assert yourself.

Alternatively, you may have made an attempt, but your voice was drowned out by a whisper when it should have been a resounding declaration.

The Permission Slip You've Been Waiting For

Let us simplify the process:

If you seek a sign, this is it.

You do not require additional qualifications, a degree, or anyone's approval.

Decide that you are sufficiently prepared and commence acting accordingly.

If an internal voice questions your legitimacy, welcome to the club. Every individual who has undertaken a daunting task has initially felt like a fraud. You cannot eliminate this voice by remaining still; you silence it through action.

Confidence and clarity are not acquired before action; they are earned through it.

Real Talk from the Other Side of the Fence

Every individual you admire—even those with millions of followers, bestselling books, or wildly successful businesses—began by declaring, "I am doing this."

They were not selected; they chose themselves.

Once they made that decision, the world adjusted.

When individuals move with certainty, they attract attention.

Therefore, I urge you to cease thinking you "deserve" opportunities. Refrain from shrinking to accommodate others. Stop waiting for your grand break.

Become your own break.

Creating Your Own Opportunities

Let us dispel the illusion that perfection is forthcoming. There is no magical email, a tap on the shoulder, or a moment when the universe grants permission to pursue your dreams.

That moment is a myth. What is tangible is this: if you seek opportunity, you create it, build it, and knock on your own door.

I understand that you have been conditioned to wait. Education instills the value of conformity, corporate life emphasises the ladder, and social media compels you to compare your chapter 1 to someone else's chapter 20.

Meanwhile, life continues unabated, and you observe it from a distance, hoping someone recognises your potential.

Newsflash: Potential holds no significance without action.

No One's Coming—And That's the Best News Ever

Contrary to popular belief, waiting for discovery can hinder your growth. Waiting to be selected can lead to stagnation, and waiting for the "perfect moment" can make you invisible.

Despite this, many individuals spend years, even decades, anticipating the mythical moment when everything aligns and feels secure.

Consider this: when was the last time an extraordinary achievement resulted from waiting?

The answer is, it has never happened.

The individuals you admire—those who take bold steps, create remarkable things, and make a significant impact—did not achieve their success by idleness. They proactively created their own opportunities. They made decisive decisions, submitted compelling proposals, and demonstrated their presence even before they felt fully prepared. They established themselves as valuable contributors, even when not formally invited to participate.

And you possess the same potential.

How to Initiate Your Own Opportunities (Immediately)

This process does not necessitate financial resources, connections, mentorship, or approval from others.

The key components are:

* **Clarity of Objectives:** Even if it is merely the next step, define your aspirations clearly.
* **Courage to Embrace Imperfection:** Embrace the fact that you may not be proficient at something until you improve.
* **Proactive Action:** Cultivate a bias towards taking action.

Here's how this principle manifests in practical scenarios:

* **Refuse to Be Invited to Speak? Host Your Own Event:** Organise a private gathering and share your insights through a video presentation. Engage in discussions proactively.
* **Unfulfilled Job Aspirations? Create a Freelance Version:** Develop a freelance version of your desired job and build a compelling portfolio to demonstrate your value.
* **Limited Opportunities? Initiate Conversations:** Approach potential connections and engage in meaningful conversations. Pose insightful questions and demonstrate your assertiveness.

For those who may be hesitant, it is crucial to remember:

* **Be Assertive and Persistent.**

From Invisibility to Unstoppable

You do not require an external platform; instead, you construct your own platform with each act of courage, consistency, and value you demonstrate.

You do not need to possess all the answers; rather, you should initiate a process of asking more pertinent questions and subsequently taking action.

Consider every opportunity you have ever admired—every company, every movement, every breakthrough. They all commenced in the same manner: an individual identified a problem, a need, or a dream and made a decision to address it.

They did not seek permission, did not wait to be prepared, nor did they await the world's approval.

They chose themselves, built it, and subsequently, the world took notice.

Permission Granted

My friend, here is your permission slip to create your own opportunity.

Once you cease waiting and commence action, everything undergoes a transformative shift. Doors open, individuals respond, confidence grows, and the previously perceived insurmountable becomes within reach.

Pursuing Your Aspirations, Even When Facing Trembling Fear

Allow me to conjecture that you possess a clear understanding of your desires, or at the very least, you have a faint glimmer of them. That elusive element that ignites your passion, that persistent concept that lingers in your mind. That version of yourself that has yet to fully manifest.

Despite this, you find yourself ensnared in a state of stagnation. Why? Because pursuing your aspirations instills an overwhelming sense of apprehension.

Naturally, it does. Naturally, it appears perilous. Naturally, it evokes vulnerability, messiness, and an abundance of hypothetical scenarios. You are not flawed; you are merely human.

However, I must confront you with an uncomfortable truth:

Fear does not signify cessation; rather, it signifies action.

Fear: A Navigational Tool, Not a Halt

When something truly holds significance for you, your brain will naturally respond with a surge of panic.

It will unleash a torrent of apprehensions: “You are not adequately prepared.” “Your knowledge is insufficient.” “What if they mock you?” “What if you fail?” “What will your family think?” “What if you achieve success but struggle to cope?”

Fear is not attempting to derail your life; rather, it serves as a protective mechanism against the inherent uncertainty of the unknown. Our brains are wired to prioritise safety over happiness. Consequently, when embarking on novel, audacious, or ambitious endeavours that surpass our previous accomplishments, our brains instinctively resist.

However, pay attention closely: the fear you experience is a clear indication that you are on the correct path.

If something truly matters, it will undoubtedly evoke a sense of trepidation. This is inherent in the process. Clarity and composure do not precede courage; rather, courage emerges first. Clarity and confidence manifest only after taking action.

The Illusion of "Someday"

Here lies the pervasive lie that perpetuates stagnation: "I will accomplish this someday, when I am prepared."

Unfortunately, this notion is unfounded.

"Preparation" is not a fleeting moment that magically materialises. It is a consequence of taking action despite fear, thereby realising that fear does not ultimately extinguish us.

The sole means of achieving a sense of readiness is to act before you feel truly prepared.

If you aspire to write a book, commence typing. If you desire to change careers, initiate networking. If you wish to express your true feelings, speak up. If you aspire to relocate across the country, commence researching neighbourhoods and making phone calls. If you intend to launch a project, cease overthinking and proceed with the launch.

You do not require additional confidence; rather, you need to make a decision.

Affirm your commitment and then take the subsequent, albeit minuscule and terrifying, step forward.

Embracing the Journey: Overcoming Fear and Achieving Your Goals

Fear can be an intimidating obstacle, but it is not insurmountable. Here are some practical strategies to navigate through it and achieve your objectives:

Acknowledge Your Fear: Begin by acknowledging the presence of your fear. Refrain from suppressing it, as it is a natural response to challenging situations.

Break Down the Task: Divide the daunting task into smaller, manageable steps. This approach makes the task less overwhelming and easier to accomplish.

Utilise Visualisation: Visualise yourself successfully completing the task. Imagine yourself taking each step with confidence and determination.

Take Action: Once you have acknowledged your fear, broken down the task, and utilised visualisation, take action. Start with the smallest step and gradually progress towards your goal.

Repeat the Process: Consistency is key. Repeat these steps as needed to overcome fear and achieve your desired outcomes.

Embrace the Journey: Remember that achieving your goals requires effort and perseverance. Embrace the journey, learn from your experiences, and stay focused on your objectives.

Overcoming Self-Doubt:

It is important to address self-doubt and negative self-talk. Replace these thoughts with positive affirmations and remind yourself of your strengths and capabilities.

Seek Support: If you are struggling to overcome self-doubt, consider seeking support from friends, family, or professionals. Sharing your feelings and receiving encouragement can be beneficial.

Practice Self-Compassion: Treat yourself with kindness and understanding, as you would a friend. Be mindful of negative self-talk and challenge those thoughts.

Embrace Personal Growth: View personal growth as an opportunity for development and improvement. Embrace challenges, learn from setbacks, and continuously strive to become better versions of yourself.

Remember, You Have the Power:

You possess the power to overcome fear and achieve your goals. Believe in yourself, take action, and embrace the journey towards success.

Feeling Stuck: A Misconception of Safety

Being stuck does not invariably evoke a sense of panic. In most instances, it manifests as a state of inaction.

Individuals may find themselves scrolling, waiting, or engaging in activities that do not yield tangible progress. These pursuits are often labelled as “preparation,” “research,” or “waiting for the opportune moment.” However, the true nature of these actions is often concealment.

Action can be daunting, as it entails relinquishing the ability to hide. It carries the risks of failure, embarrassment, and change. Nevertheless,

Stagnation poses a greater threat, as it drains time, joy, and life.

The Power of Momentum: Overcoming Motivation’s Fluctuations

Motivation is a fleeting concept, akin to a fickle companion. Its availability is unpredictable, often waning when challenges arise.

What truly propels individuals forward is momentum. This momentum originates from a single, decisive action—a defiant challenge against self-doubt or a simple 5-second decision to commence.

These actions define self-starter individuals, not rigid routines, ideal conditions, or a mere sense of readiness.

A decision, a countdown, and a move—repeat these daily, and a transformative shift occurs. Individuals cease to be passive waiters and become active movers, even amidst uncertainty, apprehension, or the absence of observers.

How to Become a Self-Starter (Even If You’ve Always Waited on Others)

Let us make this practical.

Begin your day with a win. Refrain from checking your phone and reacting immediately. Act on your own. Choose a small action, such as making your bed, taking a walk, or sending an email. By doing so, you communicate to your brain that you take action first.

Implement the Countdown practice. When an instinct arises to act on a goal, count down from 5 to 1 and take action before doubt creeps in or your brain dissuades you. This rapid rewiring of behaviour is highly effective.

Set exceedingly small goals. Instead of "run five miles," aim for "put on shoes and go outside." Similarly, instead of "write the entire chapter," focus on "opening the document and writing one sentence." Action builds confidence, and it is a consistent process.

Measure progress, not perfection. Self-starters do not wait for perfection; they begin and iterate. Starting with imperfections is significantly more powerful than waiting for perfection.

Celebrate the act, not the outcome. Confidence is not built through winning; it is cultivated through trying. Acknowledge and appreciate every brave action, especially the small ones.

Your Identity is Built by Your Actions, Not Your Thoughts

While reading books, listening to podcasts, and planning for months can be beneficial, they are meaningless if you fail to take action.

Self-starters do not possess more talent; they have more practice in embracing bravery. This process begins with a sense of being stuck, followed by taking action, and the momentum kicks in, leading to a shift in identity. You become someone who acts rather than waits.

The version of you who builds things, raises her hand, speaks up, and makes bold moves is already within you. You have simply been hindered by hesitation. Now is the time to overcome it.

No More Waiting, No More Permission, No More "Maybe Later"

You are the one you have been waiting for.

PART 4

BECOMING UNSTOPPABLE

In this pivotal section of the book, the transformative journey reaches its climax. You have diligently undertaken the arduous task of confronting and dispelling the internal deceptions, taking resolute actions, and embracing your authentic self. Now, it is imperative to fully commit to this transformative process.

Achieving a state of unwavering determination does not imply an absence of setbacks. Rather, it signifies that you have cultivated the resilience to rise from each challenge with renewed vigour, courage, and a greater alignment with your true self.

How to Fail Without Losing Yourself

Allow me to impart some unequivocal truth from the outset: If you are not experiencing failure, you are not exerting sufficient effort. Aspiring to cultivate confidence? Excellent. However, you must embrace failure with a degree of comfort, as the individuals you admire—those who excel, lead, construct, articulate their opinions, and transform their lives—have experienced more failures than you. The sole distinction lies in their willingness to acknowledge and acknowledge their failures publicly. They rise again with even greater determination.

The world does not recognise perfection; it celebrates resilience. Confidence does not develop within the confines of one's comfort zone; it emerges from the aftermath of unsuccessful endeavours. It multiplies with each decision to persist despite setbacks.

Confidence is not the absence of failure; it is the ability to rise from its ashes.

At some point, you may have been conditioned to avoid taking risks. To refrain from rocking the boat, to refrain from making mistakes, and to only pursue opportunities when you are certain of their success. This conditioning is a trap, a limitation that confines you and restricts your growth.

The most confident individuals you encounter have embraced rejection as a part of their journey. They have publicly embarrassed themselves, launched projects that failed, and spoken their minds, only to receive negative feedback and rejections. Despite these challenges, they have persevered with unwavering determination. Confidence emerges after the fall, not before it.

Hello Jessica,

The woman you encountered at the beginning of this book did not emerge from her initial encounters with confidence. She experienced a significant setback in front of her superior, panicked during a client call, and sent emails containing typographical errors. Her pitch ideas were also unsuccessful.

However, remarkably, she managed to overcome these challenges. She acknowledged her failures openly, embraced them, and moved forward. Each time she did so, the fear gradually diminished in its power.

Fear cannot hold you captive if you have demonstrated that it cannot break you.

Reframing Failure as Feedback

It is crucial to cease categorising failure as definitive. Failure is not a judgment; it is a valuable source of information.

If your pitch failed to resonate, it is beneficial to identify the areas for improvement. If you were not selected for an interview, it has eliminated potential mismatches. Even if your idea was rejected by the entire team, it provides an opportunity to recount the experience at a future success gathering.

Failure serves as an educator. By adopting a wise approach, you can transform it into a catalyst for personal growth rather than a source of shame.

I, too, have experienced numerous failures. I have shed tears in public restrooms, delivered disastrous speeches, and received criticism ranging from "too much" to "not enough." I have made errors in public settings and had to confront them the following morning.

Each of these moments strengthened me.

Not because they were pleasant, but because they prevented me from succumbing to defeat.

Resilience Through Action

Resilience is a skill, not a personality trait. Like every skill, it is developed through repeated practice.

The initial encounter with failure may prompt a desire to conceal oneself. However, with subsequent attempts, a flinching response emerges. By the tenth attempt, laughter ensues, and familiarity sets in. Failure becomes an inherent aspect of the process, and each subsequent rise demonstrates improvement.

The key principle lies in not merely bouncing back but rather propelling oneself forward.

Each time one rises, a subtle surge of courage, clarity, and evidence of resilience emerges, reinforcing the notion of overcoming adversity.

The Truth About Rejection, Criticism, and Setbacks

Let us confront the harsh reality that individuals are prone to judgment regardless of circumstances. Criticism is inevitable, whether proactive or passive. Rejection is an inherent component of life.

Why, then, do individuals succumb to its paralysing effects?

The common response is self-pre-rejection. Individuals refrain from expressing themselves, applying for opportunities, taking action, or asking for assistance due to the apprehension of receiving a negative response.

However, confidence does not stem from avoiding rejection; it arises from acknowledging one's ability to endure it.

One can endure the disapproval of a post, the neglect of a job application, or the dismissal of a significant idea.

The moment one demonstrates to oneself that rejection does not diminish their worth is the pivotal juncture.

At this juncture, an unstoppable force emerges.

No longer is there a pursuit of safety; instead, the focus shifts to growth. This growth is the foundation upon which genuine confidence is constructed—not in the planning phase, but in the face of challenges.

Fail. Loudly.

Here's your challenge: cease attempting to conceal the mess. Cease pretending that you have it all figured out. Embrace failure, loudly, boldly, and repeatedly.

Pose the question. Present the idea. Initiate the task.

Should you encounter a setback? Should you faceplant in front of everyone?

Rise again. Own it. Laugh if you can. Learn from it. Then repeat the process.

For the individuals who achieve success in life are not those who play it safe.

They are the ones who endeavoured, failed, adjusted, and persisted.

You possess the potential for a comeback. Therefore, make the error and then take action.

Confidence is not the absence of failure; it is the ability to rise after it.

Let us dispel the misconceptions: You have been misled.

Somewhere along the way, you began to believe that confident individuals do not make mistakes. That they consistently possess the right words, never stumble, consistently secure opportunities, and exude certainty as if it were an inherent trait.

That notion is erroneous.

Confidence does not entail consistently achieving success. It entails recognising that when you fail, you have the resilience to recover.

The most influential individuals in the room have publicly, painfully, and repeatedly experienced setbacks. The sole distinction is that they did not allow these failures to define them.

Do you believe that the CEO has never experienced a pitch failure? Do you believe that the speaker has never experienced a stage fright? Do you believe that the bestselling author has never received a hundred rejections?

Please.

The individuals you most admire are not fearless. They are resilient. They have acquired a valuable lesson that most people never do:

Confidence is nurtured in the moments following failure.

Not before. Not when everything proceeds flawlessly. But when the meeting falters, your voice wavers, the email contains a typographical error, you bomb the interview—and instead of succumbing to defeat, you decide to return.

That is where confidence resides: in the act of rising.

The Fork in the Road

Failure is an inevitable part of the human experience, and it presents us with a critical juncture. Imagine encountering a fork in the road, with one path leading to shame, self-doubt, and the belief that you are not suited for the task. Conversely, the other path offers the opportunity for growth and development.

The immediate aftermath of failure marks a pivotal moment in our lives. It is at this juncture that our future is shaped, not by the severity of the setback, but by our response to it.

At this juncture, we have two choices: succumb to the inner critic and retreat, or take a deep breath, maintain composure, and resume our pursuit of success.

Observing a toddler learning to walk provides a poignant illustration of this principle. Despite numerous falls, face-first, the toddler remains resolute. They do not allow these setbacks to define their worth or discourage their efforts. Instead, they rise again and again until they achieve the remarkable feat of running.

Somewhere along the way, we tend to lose this resilience. We begin to assign significance to our failures, interpreting them as indicators of inadequacy, exclusion, or a call to surrender. However, these interpretations are misguided. Failure is merely a natural part of the learning process, a testament to our humanity, and a reminder of our vitality.

Embrace the Fall: A Pathway to Confidence

If you are hesitant to take risks, fearing failure, you will find yourself perpetually waiting.

Remember, confidence does not derive from consistently succeeding. It arises from embracing fear, experiencing setbacks, and recognising that you persist.

Failure is not an adversary; avoiding it is.

When you shun risk, you also deny yourself opportunities for growth. Without growth, confidence eludes you.

Therefore, embrace failure with audacity and unapologetic honesty. Allow others to observe and speculate.

For when you rise after they anticipate your downfall, that embodies true power.

The Essence of Confidence: Overcoming Failure

The fundamental principle is that confidence is not built upon avoiding failure. Instead, it is forged through demonstrating repeatedly that failure cannot impede your progress.

Therefore, the next time you encounter a setback, remember that your confidence lies not in the perfection of your landing but in the courage with which you rise.

Reframing Failure as Feedback

To be unequivocal, failure is not a definitive judgment. It serves as valuable data.

It is not evidence of inadequacy nor a clear indication of inadequacy. Rather, it presents a clue, a piece of evidence, within the intricate and imperfect journey of human growth.

However, many individuals perceive failure as the culmination of their path.

For instance, after a presentation that fails to impress, they may conclude, "I lack leadership abilities." Similarly, a pitch that fails to generate enthusiasm may lead them to assert, "I am incapable of creativity." Furthermore, a rejection can prompt them to refrain from putting themselves out there again.

These reactions are not constructive feedback; they are self-destructive rationalisations.

The truth is that every failure presents an opportunity for learning and development. Most of us are too preoccupied with self-criticism to perceive these lessons.

Failure is Not Personal; It is Informational

When an infant attempts to walk and fails, we do not label it a failure. Instead, we acknowledge it as a learning experience.

However, when we undertake significant endeavours, such as launching a business, commencing a podcast, or expressing romantic interest in someone, and the outcome deviates from our expectations, we often resort to self-deprecating statements like, "I am not suited for this."

This mindset is erroneous.

The fundamental principle remains the same. Our cognitive processes have been shaped by years of perfectionism, people-pleasing, and the apprehension of appearing foolish.

To break this cycle, we must adopt an engineer's perspective when examining failures. If the initial version of a prototype fails, it is not a cause for alarm. Instead, we identify the specific aspects that malfunctioned, the necessary adjustments, and the valuable lessons learned.

Engineers do not abandon their projects due to the shortcomings of the first version. They refine their approach, iteratively improving each subsequent version until they achieve the desired outcome, which is often hailed as genius.

The same principle applies to building confidence.

Reframing the Experience

Consider a scenario where you deliver a speech and experience a moment of blankness during the middle section.

One possible response would be to self-criticise, "I am utterly incompetent at public speaking. I embarrassed myself. I will never engage in such activities again."

Alternatively, you could reframe the situation by acknowledging that you lacked adequate preparation. In the future, you will dedicate more time to practicing the middle section. Furthermore, you can acknowledge that you survived the experience and will continue to improve.

The same event can yield vastly different interpretations. The second approach fosters confidence, while the first approach can be detrimental to self-esteem.

The key factor lies not in the specific events themselves but in the self-perceptions we construct based on those events.

Feedback: A Catalyst for Growth

To achieve success in any endeavour, it is imperative to seek more feedback. However, feedback is most effective when accompanied by a willingness to:

- Maintain an open mindset, even when it involves constructive criticism.
- Detach one's identity from their performance evaluations.
- Utilise feedback as a means of adjustment rather than retreating from challenges.

A notable example is Jessica, encountered in Chapter 1, who gained confidence not through a single successful meeting, but through a series of unsuccessful ones. Each failure provided valuable insights, opportunities for learning, and a chance to adjust and improve.

Failures should not be perceived as obstacles; instead, they serve as signposts that guide us forward. By reading and applying these lessons, we can move beyond setbacks and progress toward our goals.

Embracing Failure as a Growth Opportunity

Adopt a new mantra: "I do not fail; I collect data."

Practice this mantra by verbalising it when a situation does not yield the desired outcome. This act can disrupt the negative cycle and redirect your focus toward personal growth.

Reframing failure as feedback has a transformative effect: it diminishes fear and empowers individuals to overcome challenges.

Building Resilience Through Action

Contrary to popular belief, resilience is not a passive state of mind; it is cultivated through consistent action. Instead of dwelling on the concept of resilience, focus on taking proactive steps to overcome obstacles.

Engage in action, even when faced with apprehension or fear. This proactive approach is essential for building resilience and achieving long-term success.

Rock Bottom: A Turning Point

The experience of experiencing a series of setbacks, such as a failed plan, a missed opportunity, or a rejection email, can be disheartening. However, it is important to recognise that these moments are not the culmination of one's journey; rather, they serve as pivotal junctures that can lead to a resurgence of strength and determination.

Resilience is not an innate trait but a skill that can be cultivated through consistent effort. It is not about avoiding challenges but rather about developing the ability to bounce back from adversity. When faced with a setback, it is crucial to maintain a positive outlook and acknowledge the value of the experience.

Resilience is built through action. It is the process of overcoming obstacles and pushing through resistance. Each time we rise above a challenge, we reinforce our ability to handle difficult situations. This process is particularly effective when accompanied by self-affirmations that reinforce our resilience.

While verbal affirmations can be beneficial, they are not sufficient on their own. True resilience requires action and the willingness to confront discomfort. By engaging in challenging activities, we can reinforce our belief in our ability to overcome obstacles.

In essence, resilience is not a matter of being unbroken; it is about developing the strength and determination to overcome setbacks and build a more fulfilling life. By demonstrating resilience through our actions, we can empower ourselves to achieve our goals and overcome any obstacle that arises.

The Scientific Basis of Resilient Action

Engaging in action, even seemingly insignificant or imperfect actions, activates the prefrontal cortex, the brain region responsible for decision-making and strategic planning. This activation overrides the amygdala, which typically triggers a fight-or-flight response. By doing so, individuals can cease reacting and respond appropriately, effectively calming turbulent situations.

Therefore, taking action, regardless of its perceived readiness, is more crucial than waiting for a perceived state of perfection. It is important to recognise that initial action is often the foundation upon which strength emerges.

Case Study: Rachel

Consider Rachel, Jessica's colleague who exuded an aura of polish and perfection. However, beneath her composed exterior lay a tumultuous year marked by divorce, job loss, and financial difficulties.

Rachel did not resort to meditation or seek magical solutions. Instead, she rose each day, shed tears in the shower, and persisted in her responsibilities. She began by embracing challenging tasks and expressing willingness to try new things. Seeking assistance, she embarked on a freelance gig, honed new skills, and meticulously rebuilt her life, one uncomfortable step at a time.

Resilience, in its essence, may not be aesthetically pleasing, but it embodies unwavering strength. It manifests in the form of determination, perseverance, and the willingness to confront adversity head-on.

Action > Answers

You do not need to possess the entire path. You do not require a decade-long plan.

You merely need your next step.

Not flawless, not guaranteed, but something—a single step forward.

Resilience is not merely about bouncing back; it is about propelling forward—because you have undergone a transformation.

Therefore, cease waiting to feel courageous. Cease attempting to identify the ideal moment.

Take action.

Apply for the job. Initiate the phone call. Open the gym door. Speak up. Send the message. Persist.

Resilience resides not within your mind, but in your subsequent action.

And if you aspire to feel more resilient, act with greater strength. Your mind will eventually catch up.

The Truth About Rejection, Criticism, and Setbacks

Let us confront the reality:

You will encounter rejection. You will receive criticism. You will face setbacks.

These are not flaws in your journey; they are inherent aspects of it.

The sooner you cease internalising these experiences, the sooner you will progress.

Rejection Does Not Indicate Lack of Sufficient Qualifications

Rejection can evoke a sense of being scrutinised and dismissed.

It is akin to someone peering into your aspirations and expressing disdain.

When such an experience occurs, it is natural to conclude that you are not worthy.

However, the truth is:

Rejection is never a reflection of your inherent value. It is often a matter of alignment, timing, or apprehension on their part.

Occasionally, the opportunity presented itself at an inopportune moment. Sometimes, the other individual failed to perceive your potential. In other instances, they were simply experiencing a challenging day and took it out on you.

Their negative response does not diminish your worth.

It is not a judgment; it is merely a data point.

If you utilise this data to adjust your trajectory and continue moving forward, you will ultimately emerge victorious.

Criticism is an inherent aspect of human interaction, and it is not always directed at oneself.

When undertaking bold actions, such as writing a post, pitching an idea, wearing a new outfit, or expressing one's true thoughts, it is inevitable that criticism will arise. Individuals often criticise those they do not understand, judge what makes them uncomfortable, and project their own insecurities onto those who dare to shine.

Before absorbing criticism, it is crucial to pause and reflect on the following questions:

- Is the criticism directed at me or at the subject matter?
- Do they genuinely know me?
- Do they live a life that I admire?

Remember, individuals who sit on the sidelines, voicing negativity while others strive for success, do not possess a valid vote.

It is advisable to seek guidance from individuals who are genuinely supportive and who would not trade lives with you. Therefore, it is equally important to refrain from accepting criticism from such individuals.

Setbacks are not the culmination of one's journey; rather, they are an integral part of the process of growth and development.

To achieve a strong physique, one engages in weightlifting. Similarly, to build a confident life, one must confront and overcome setbacks.

The same principle applies to various aspects of life. Aspiring for a dream job may involve rejection, while building a relationship entails awkward conversations, vulnerability, and heartbreak. Launching a business entails mistakes, stumbles, and occasional slowdowns.

Setbacks should not be perceived as obstacles; rather, they serve as training opportunities. They instil resilience, clarity, and a sense of what truly matters.

Individuals who admire and excel in their endeavours have likely experienced more failures than they have attempted. The distinction lies in their unwavering determination and ability to transform their pain into fuel for success.

What If You Refrained from Taking Rejections Personally?

Consider this: What actions would you take today if you were certain that you could not take rejections personally?

That negative response would not diminish your abilities.
The silence following your presentation was not a rejection, merely a delay.
The sarcastic comment on your post revealed more about them than you.

Confidence arises from embracing the potential for setbacks and demonstrating your commitment regardless.

Adopt a mindset of, "This may not be successful—but I am pursuing it anyway."

The only way to cultivate such unwavering confidence is to repeatedly confront rejection, criticism, and challenges until you comprehend: These obstacles do not define you; they shape and refine you.

Therefore, proceed with your endeavours. Share your content, express your opinions, present your ideas, and take risks.

Allow them to underestimate you, criticise your efforts, and reject your requests.

Your actions are not driven by their approval; they are motivated by the desire to provide a better future for your future self.

How to Be Loud Enough as You Are

At a pivotal moment—sometimes after a breakup, sometimes in a boardroom, or even while brushing your teeth at 6 AM—you may look in the mirror and realise that you have been exhausted by trying to conform to others' expectations.

That moment, that is the catalyst. That is the beginning of your journey towards reclaiming your life.

Here is the unvarnished, liberating truth:

You do not need to raise your voice. You merely need to be authentic.

Reclaiming Your Voice

I presume you have spent years suppressing your voice.

Perhaps it began in school, where being intellectually gifted made you a target. Or at home, where your ambitious aspirations made someone else feel uncomfortable. Or in meetings, where you have observed someone with half your insight speak up with twice your confidence and receive praise for it.

Your silence did not manifest overnight. It was a gradual demise through a multitude of silent acquiescences.

However, your voice is not entirely absent. It lies concealed beneath politeness, “What will they think?” and layers of performing for approval.

Reclaiming it does not imply becoming someone you are not—it entails returning to your original self before the world dictated that you should shrink.

The “you” who was vocal with laughter, curious, bold, messy, and honest.

That voice? It persists, awaiting your permission to express yourself once more.

Confidence as Alignment—Not Performance

Confidence is not about being the most vocal individual in a room; it is about aligning oneself with one’s true self.

Individuals can discern a facade from a distance, but when one speaks from a place of authenticity, their words resonate deeply.

When one’s inner voice harmonises with their external words, they enter a room and evoke a profound response, not through performance, but through their presence.

This shift from a state of seeking approval to a position of ownership fosters confidence.

The authentic version of oneself radiates confidence, not perfection or polish, but rather alignment.

Emotional Safety, Authenticity, and Peace of Mind

Peace of mind cannot be purchased; it is a liberating experience.

Waking up without the need to don a costume is liberating. There is no longer a need to project a specific persona, such as the "cool" one, the "chill" one, or the "tough" one. There is no more self-doubt over every text message. There is no longer a need to conform to the expectations of others.

Authenticity embodies the highest form of self-respect. It serves as an effective defence against burnout, resentment, and imposter syndrome.

When one lives in alignment with their true self, expressing "yes" when they mean "no" and smiling while struggling internally, they betray themselves for fleeting approval.

This state of being is not peace; it is survival.

True confidence arises from embracing one's identity, beliefs, and aspirations, without the need for apology.

Embracing Authenticity: Living Your Truth Unapologetically

Contrary to popular belief, being disliked is more challenging than appearing artificial and gaining popularity through deception.

You were not born to navigate life in a manner that appeases everyone while neglecting your own well-being. Your purpose lies in expressing yourself authentically, creating, leading, connecting, and disrupting the world in your unique way.

This authenticity should not be compromised; it should be fully embraced. It may entail confronting discomfort and potential rejection, but it is essential for personal growth and fulfilment.

The moment you cease conforming to external expectations, the right individuals will emerge, and opportunities will arise. Moreover, you will attain a profound sense of wholeness.

You will no longer be reliant on external validation or managing the perceptions of others. You will simply be yourself.

And that, my friend, is far more powerful than any performance ever could be.

Reclaiming Your Authenticity

It is crucial to recognise that you were never "too much." Rather, you were surrounded by individuals who struggled to comprehend your brilliance, enthusiasm, and assertiveness.

As a result, you gradually diminished your presence, not out of a conscious choice, but because it felt safer at some point. It could have been the influence of a teacher who criticised your talkativeness, a first boss who suppressed your ideas, or a parent who labeled you as "dramatic" during emotional moments.

Over time, you internalised the notion that being quieter, smaller, and agreeable made you more acceptable. Consequently, you began filtering your thoughts before speaking, transforming bold ideas into cautious inquiries. You allowed interruptions and overrides, convinced that you were merely being "polite."

However, the truth remains: the voice you have been suppressing is still present. It has not vanished; it has merely been concealed beneath years of attempting to maintain harmony, gain popularity, and avoid conflict.

Rather than seeking to discover your voice, you must reclaim it.

Reclaiming Your Voice: A Journey to Self-Expression

Reclaiming your voice begins with a profound question:

"When did I cease to express myself?"

Was it a fleeting moment, a recurring pattern, or a strained relationship? Investigate these factors in depth.

Reflect on the last occasion when you refrained from conveying your true thoughts. Perhaps it was during a meeting, with your partner, or when you desired to contribute, propose an idea, or express your dissent but hesitated.

Your silence was not the root cause; rather, the self-perception you cultivated surrounding it was.

You may have internalised the following thoughts:

"I will accumulate more experience before speaking up."
"The present moment is not opportune."
"They will disregard my input regardless."

However, consider the potential consequences of simply expressing yourself.

What if the world remained unchanged, yet instead, it expanded?

Reclaiming: Not Always Aggressive

It is essential to dispel the misconception that reclaiming your voice entails shouting from a platform or causing disruption.

In some instances, reclaiming your voice entails:

Communicating your genuine feelings to your partner.
Asserting your boundaries without seeking apology.
Granting yourself permission to be vulnerable, honest, and emotionally expressive.

It involves choosing to be perceived, even when your voice trembles.

It entails trusting your ideas, even if they do not garner applause.

It entails speaking for yourself, not against others.

Aggression is not a prerequisite; clarity is.

Loudness is not necessary; authenticity is.

Practice Speaking Out Loud

Here's your challenge: Practice using your voice in safe, everyday situations.

Speak up in a group chat when you would normally remain silent.
Express your disagreement in a meeting instead of acquiescing.
Inform the waiter that your order has been incorrect (even that counts).
Request what you want, even if it feels "too much."

Each time you use your voice—even in small ways—you reinforce this truth in your mind:

"My thoughts matter."

And you know what? They do.

Embrace Your Inner Voice

Don't wait until you feel "ready." That's fear disguised as logic.

Confidence doesn't manifest before you speak. It emerges after—when you demonstrate to yourself that you are still standing.

Therefore, cease waiting for permission. Cease waiting for the opportune moment. Cease editing yourself for approval.

You have something to express. The world does not require another echo.

It needs your truth.

Speak it. Even if your voice trembles. Especially then.

That is how you reclaim it. That is how you return to yourself. And that is how the authentic you emerges—on your own terms.

Confidence as Alignment, Not Performance

Let us dispel the misconceptions: most of us believe confidence is a performance.

We perceive it as the manner in which someone enters a room with an air of ownership, delivers a compelling presentation, dominates the conversation, exudes a polished smile, and consistently lacks self-doubt.

However, I must reveal a liberating truth:

That is not confidence. That is a performance.

Performances are exhausting. They are high-maintenance, reliant on applause, and perpetually on the verge of collapse once the spotlight ceases.

True confidence is not something you adorn; it is something you align—from within.

It is alignment.

What is Alignment, Really?

Alignment refers to the alignment of one's actions with their values. One's choices reflect their authenticity, and their words resonate with their genuine voice rather than a pre-fabricated version.

When aligned, there is no need to project confidence; one naturally embodies it because there is no conflict between their inner self and their outward expression.

Alignment exudes a sense of tranquility, power, and sustainability. It occurs when the inner and outer worlds finally harmonise.

It is crucial to recognise that one is not performing for a job, a date, or a family. Instead, one should simply be themselves—fully, clearly, and without apology.

This authenticity possesses a magnetic allure.

The Peril of Performed Confidence

Performed confidence is a common practice, often taught in various contexts. While tips such as "stand tall," "speak louder," and "fake it till you make it" may provide temporary assistance in situations like presentations or interviews, they lack the foundation of alignment.

Confidence derived from alignment is ultimately hollow and can lead to feelings of fraud, a lack of authenticity, and constant exhaustion. Pretending and masking are exhausting endeavours, and performing constantly seeks approval rather than standing in one's truth.

Alignment: Acting in Harmony with Your Inner Truth

Alignment is the silent power of self-awareness and consistent action. It allows you to assert your boundaries without guilt, leave a job that no longer aligns with your values, and embrace a new beginning driven by intuition rather than fear.

Alignment ensures that your external life reflects your inner truth. It means living authentically, without pre-written scripts or costumes. You become clear, grounded, and whole.

Transitioning from Performance to Alignment

1. **Identify Misalignment:** Be honest with yourself about any discomfort or inconsistencies. Are you agreeing to commitments when you don't truly want to? Are you presenting a different version of yourself to others while living a different life? Your discomfort serves as a compass, guiding you towards areas of misalignment.

2. **Define Your Confidence:** Clarify what confidence means to you. It may manifest as peace, truthfulness, or boldness without being assertive. Your definition of confidence should be unique to you.

3. **Align Your Actions:** Begin aligning your actions, even with small steps. Wear the clothes that make you feel comfortable, speak the truth you have been holding back, and set boundaries, even if your voice trembles. These incremental movements towards alignment build substantial confidence.

4. **Pay Attention to Energy:** When you are aligned, you feel lighter, even in challenging situations. Conversely, when you are performing, you experience tension, fatigue, and a constant need for validation.

Embrace Authenticity: Refrain from Seeking Approval from Uninformed Individuals

It is undeniable that some individuals are drawn to the easily accessible, reserved, and agreeable aspects of your personality.

However, it is crucial to recognise that this is their prerogative. Your primary objective should not be to ensure the comfort of others. Instead, focus on being authentic and allowing the right individuals to connect with you.

Confidence derived from performance is inherently fragile, while confidence rooted in alignment is unshakable. By ceasing to constantly monitor your actions to ascertain whether you are "doing it right" and abandoning the pursuit of universal approval, you will cultivate a profound sense of self-assurance.

Embrace Alignment: Authenticity and Emotional Well-being

One aspect that is often overlooked but essential for personal growth is emotional safety.

Have you ever entered a room and immediately perceived judgmental glances? Have you suppressed your opinions to avoid disrupting the status quo? Have you resorted to humour that caused discomfort merely to conform?

These behaviours indicate a prioritisation of survival over authenticity.

It is imperative to recognise that you deserve more than mere survival. You are entitled to feel emotionally safe in your own skin, in your interactions, in your relationships, and in every aspect of your life.

What Is Emotional Safety, Really?

Emotional safety is not a mere buzzword or a superficial self-help concept. It is the bedrock upon which individuals can function effectively, develop confidence, and express themselves fully.

Emotional safety entails the ability to communicate one's thoughts and feelings freely without fear of reprisal, ridicule, or abandonment. It means being authentic and genuine without resorting to self-deception or conforming to societal expectations.

Without emotional safety, individuals tend to shrink inward, build defensive barriers, and constantly second-guess their actions, ideas, and emotions. This constant state of anxiety hinders the development of confidence, as it is difficult to be bold and assertive when one is perpetually on edge.

The Link Between Safety and Authenticity

It is crucial to clarify that authenticity is not a fixed personality trait. Rather, it is a conscious decision and a practice that requires a safe and supportive environment.

Consider the following scenarios: would you be comfortable sharing your truth with someone who subsequently uses it against you? Would you be able to fully engage in a workplace where mistakes are penalised? Would you feel comfortable being vulnerable in a relationship where silence is perceived as punishment?

Clearly, the answer to these questions is negative. Therefore, it is essential to create an inner world that is robust, self-trusting, and conducive to emotional safety.

True confidence manifests in the knowledge that even when the external environment may not feel safe, one possesses a sense of self-assurance and well-being.

How to Establish Emotional Safety (Even If You Have Never Experienced It)

1. **Cease Self-Gaslighting:** Identify and acknowledge your gut feelings, moments of discomfort, or instances when you deliberately diminished your presence to avoid conflict. Refrain from dismissing these experiences as insignificant. Validate your own experiences.

2. **Prioritise Honesty:** Maintain honesty, even if it entails vulnerability or awkwardness. The more you communicate truthfully with yourself and others, the stronger your sense of inner security becomes.

3. **Release the Desire for Universal Acceptance:** Understand that you are not universally liked, and attempting to be will inevitably compromise your peace of mind.

4. **Establish Boundaries as a Priority:** Boundaries serve as the foundation of safety, defining the boundaries between personal space and external interactions. If someone disregards your boundaries, it should be their cue to depart.

What True Peace of Mind Encompasses

Visualise waking up without dreading your inbox. Imagine dining without replaying every conversation. Imagine posting, speaking truthfully, wearing your outfit, commencing a project, and not harbouring self-doubt for days.

This is the essence of peace of mind. Contrary to popular belief, it is not an exclusive state reserved for monks or influencers. It is accessible to all.

However, it is essential to acknowledge that achieving peace of mind comes at a cost—the relinquishment of an approval addiction.

You must cease seeking validation from individuals who only appreciate the version of yourself that conforms to societal expectations.

You must be prepared to disappoint others to prevent self-disappointment.

Above all, you must prioritise your authenticity over the pursuit of comfort.

Authenticity is not about being loud; it is about being clear.

You do not need to shout to be heard. You do not need to post your entire life to prove your authenticity. You do not need to explain your choices to those who do not experience the consequences.

Authenticity is a quiet revolution.

It involves wearing what feels true to you. It involves taking the path that makes no sense to anyone but your soul. It involves saying no with a smile and not offering a single apology.

And the most remarkable aspect? Once you begin living this way, your peace of mind significantly improves.

You sleep better. You breathe easier. You cease rehearsing your life and start living it fully.

Final Truth: Confidence Grows in a Safe Environment

Confidence does not grow in perfection, constant rightness, or unanimous agreement.

Confidence grows in a safe space where you feel comfortable being authentic, acknowledging your mistakes, and embracing your true self.

This is precisely what we are striving to create here.

Not a mask, not a brand, not a highlight reel.

A life where you can finally exhale and live authentically.

Living Your Truth Unapologetically

Let us address the elephant in the room: You were not born to blend in.

You were not placed on this planet to navigate people's comfort zones. You were not designed to conceal your ideas, your voice, your instincts, or your unique, extraordinary, and imperfect truth solely to maintain peace.

Yet, unfortunately, many of us are succumbing to this pattern.

We edit ourselves in conversations. We moderate our opinions. We remain in jobs we despise, relationships that drain us, and routines that gradually suffocate us—all in an attempt to avoid judgment, disappointment, or the discomfort of being our true selves.

However, it is crucial to recognise that this "comfort" you cling to is actually detrimental to your well-being.

Why Most People Never Live Their Truth

Honesty is often the most challenging path to follow. It is easier to conform to societal norms and avoid the potential for criticism or rejection. It is simpler to express consent when one intends to deny it rather than confront the disappointment of others. It is more comfortable to remain silent, stagnant, and secure.

Truth, however, can be disruptive. It compels change, challenges preconceived notions, and can even rattle one's own sense of self. Suppressing one's authentic self, however, can lead to a profound sense of disconnection and a loss of self-awareness.

This, my friend, is the most silent form of tragedy.

Living Loud Isn't About Being Aggressive—It's About Being Aligned

It is essential to clarify that living one's truth unapologetically does not imply aggressive behaviour or excessive noise. It signifies a deep understanding of one's identity and a sense of self-assurance that allows for independent standing.

True alignment prioritises personal values and inner peace over external approval. It involves trusting one's intuition, honouring one's energy, and communicating one's intentions without the need for excessive explanation.

The most crucial realisation for many individuals is that they do not owe anyone an apology for their authentic self, provided that their actions do not cause harm to others.

What Authenticity Appears Like in Real Life

It manifests as declining a party due to the necessity of rest, rather than resorting to deception.

It involves embracing bold lipstick, vibrant sneakers, and a sharp suit, because they align with your true self.

It entails presenting an idea in a meeting despite trembling voice.

It entails leaving a job, a relationship, or a narrative that no longer resonates with you, even if others fail to comprehend.

It is not an effortless path, but it is undoubtedly worthwhile. When you live your truth unapologetically, you cease to externalise your self-worth.

You begin living from within, rather than relying on external influences.

Unapologetic Does Not Equate to Unkindness

Let us delve into nuance.

Living unapologetically does not grant permission to be impolite. It is not about disregarding boundaries or ignoring repercussions.

It embodies integrity. It involves owning your truth and allowing others to own theirs. It signifies finally breaking free from the mental confinement that dictates, “I cannot express this,” “I cannot embody that,” or “I will lose them if I change.”

Pay attention closely: If you lose individuals by being honest, grounded, and authentic… They were never truly a part of your life.

Your Truth Is Not Too Loud

If your truth causes discomfort, it does not imply that you are excessive. It simply indicates that they are not yet prepared for it. This is acceptable. You are not responsible for guiding someone else’s development; you are solely focused on your own growth.

Therefore, raise your voice.

Speak from your heart, live with clarity, and assert yourself.

There is nothing more powerful than an individual who has finally achieved inner peace.

Final Thought: If It Demands Your Peace, It Is Excessive

The world does not require another carbon copy. It does not necessitate further diluted versions of truth.

It requires you—authentic, raw, and fully present.

For when you live your truth unreservedly, you grant the individuals around you the permission to do the same.

You become the signal, not the echo.

And that is how we transform the game—not solely for ourselves, but for everyone observing.

Therefore, cease self-editing, dim your light, and refrain from apologising for matters that are not incorrect.

Be who you truly are, express yourself openly, purposefully, and fully engaged.

How to Build the Brave Future You Deserve

Let us clarify one fundamental aspect: your future is not an automatic occurrence. It is not a prize bestowed upon the fortunate few, a lottery ticket that may be won through kindness, patience, or relentless effort, or a reward for possessing complete mastery.

Rather, it is a conscious choice.

A thousand choices, accumulated day after day. The sooner you acknowledge that your future is within your control—not your past, not your apprehension, nor your critics—the sooner you can commence constructing a tangible reality.

Let us contemplate the future you—the one who awakens with enthusiasm, who takes action, speaks up, and does not succumb to timidity. The one who finally pursues their aspirations—not in the distant future, but in the present moment.

The question is not whether you possess the potential to become that person; rather, it is whether you possess the courage to construct it.

Visualisation as Activation

Let us commence with an approach that may initially appear esoteric, yet it is not.

Visualisation.

I understand that you are familiar with this concept, perhaps even have experimented with it. You may have closed your eyes, envisioned your ideal lifestyle, created a vision board, or imagined sipping champagne on a yacht.

However, my intention is not to introduce a mere fantasy. Rather, I propose employing visualisation as a tool akin to an athlete preparing for a race, a speaker preparing for a stage performance, or a pilot reviewing a flight checklist. This is not a mere escapade; it is mental rehearsal.

When you visualise yourself taking action, your brain begins to establish that future as a viable possibility.

Let us provide specific examples:
- Do not merely envision yourself winning; envision yourself initiating the action.
- Visualise yourself sending the email, making the call, requesting the meeting.
- Visualise yourself entering the room, presenting your idea, and publishing it.

The reason behind this approach lies in the fact that your brain cannot distinguish between vividly imagined events and actual occurrences. This phenomenon is not mere spiritual embellishment; it is a scientific phenomenon.

Visualisation activates the brain's decision-making and focus centres. Consequently, instead of passively hoping that the future will find you, you actively embark on a purposeful journey towards it.

Setting Bold, Aligned Goals

Most individuals do not set goals; they merely express aspirations. They utter statements such as, “I aspire to lose weight,” “I desire to establish a business,” or “It would be gratifying to compose a book.” Subsequently, they remain idly by.

However, genuine goals entail decisions.

Furthermore, they necessitate alignment.

A compelling, aligned goal manifests as follows:

“My objective is to cultivate physical strength, necessitating the consistent lifting of weights three times per week.”
“My aspiration is to gain autonomy over my time, which I will achieve through freelancing by December.”
“My aspiration is to engage in public speaking, which I will accomplish by emailing five event organisers this month.”

Observe the distinction.

A wish awaits the auspicious alignment of circumstances. A goal aligns you with the aspirations you aspire to attain.

Furthermore, the most crucial revelation most individuals refrain from sharing is that it is acceptable for your goals to evoke a sense of trepidation. They should. This apprehension signifies that they are challenging you to grow. The key lies not in feeling courageous prior to commencing action, but rather in taking action nonetheless.

Becoming the Individual Who Guides Your Life

Allow me to convey a message that is imperative for your understanding:

No one will come to your rescue.

I do not assert this with malice; rather, I emphasise it because the moment you acknowledge this truth is the moment your power returns.

You have dedicated an excessive amount of time to waiting for the green light, the opportune moment, permission, or someone to select, recognise, and present you with an opportunity.

It is time to cease this passive state.

The future you envision will not materialise unless you actively contribute.

This implies that you must cease reacting and embrace leadership. You must cease blaming and commence constructing. You must cease scrolling, doubting, and hesitating, and instead, take action.

You become the individual who initiates the movement, rather than the one who awaits an invitation.

This does not imply that you must embark on a full-fledged journey overnight. Instead, you must establish momentum through small, courageous decisions made each and every day.

This is how confidence is cultivated, legacies are forged, and futures are reshaped.

The Final Push: Your Confidence Manifesto

You have overcome the challenges that held you back. You have endured the doubts, discomfort, and excuses that sought to limit your potential.

Now, it is time to transform your mindset and achieve your goals.

I challenge you to compose your Confidence Manifesto.

Do not delay; write now. Express your beliefs, aspirations, and the boundaries you have set for yourself. Reflect on your actions, even if they evoke fear. This manifesto serves as a personal contract with yourself.

If you require inspiration, consider the following prompt:

“I am no longer waiting for readiness. I take action before self-doubt hinders me. I trust my inner wisdom to guide me. I do not require permission; I possess the courage to pursue my goals. I am not inadequate; I am precisely sufficient. I live boldly, demonstrating my presence and taking initiative.

“Reflect on this manifesto daily. Speak its words aloud when needed. Use it as a reminder that you are not accumulating confidence for its own sake. Instead, you are cultivating confidence to achieve the life you truly desire.”

Final Thought: Embracing the Beginning

The future you envision may not be mapped out, but it does possess a compass—and you possess it.

You possess the necessary tools, the unwavering determination, and the profound truth within you, even if it may still be a whisper.

Now, it is time to embody that truth in your actions.

Confidence is not a fleeting emotion; it is a tangible presence that emerges from taking courageous, honest steps, even if they may be messy and uncertain.

Therefore, take action. Construct your life, embark on a journey of self-discovery, and commence anew.

Your future awaits, and you possess the courage to seize it.

Setting Clear and Purposeful Goals

Let us clarify a fundamental aspect: You do not require additional goals.

Rather, you need more ambitious goals—goals that challenge you and stretch your capabilities. However, most importantly, you should align these goals with your authentic self, rather than conforming to societal expectations.

Many intelligent and driven individuals fall into a common trap: they construct a life that appears satisfactory on paper but feels hollow and unsatisfying on the inside. They tick off the necessary accomplishments, collect the accolades, ascend the ladder, yet still grapple with feelings of anxiety and emptiness.

This state is not driven by ambition; it is a disconnect from oneself.

Therefore, let us take a moment to be candid: what truly desires you? Not the aspirations of your superiors, the expectations of your parents, nor the superficial allure of social media.

You.

If you pause at this juncture and find yourself at a loss for words, then that is precisely where we begin. Clarity invariably emerges from honesty.

A bold goal without alignment can lead to burnout. Conversely, a bold goal aligned with your authentic self can ignite a transformative force within you.

Here's a simple framework to help you find a meaningful goal:

1. **Begin with Energy:**
Reflect on the past few months and identify the moments when you felt most alive and fulfilled. These were likely moments when you were engaged in activities such as creating something, coaching others, speaking up, building something, taking risks, or serving others. These experiences serve as your compass.

2. **Align with Your Values:**
A goal that aligns with your values will motivate you without compromising your principles. It will require courage, not compromise.

Ask yourself:
- Does this goal reflect my core values?
- Am I proud of the underlying reasons behind this goal?

- Would I pursue this goal even if no one was observing?

3. **Make it Specific and Challenging:**
Vague goals lack the necessary motivation to drive action. Instead of vague statements like “I want to be more confident,” specify your goals clearly. For instance, you could say, “I want to pitch my startup on stage by December.” Similarly, instead of “I want to be healthier,” you could say, “I am committed to running a half marathon in six months.”

The ideal goal should stretch your belief system and foster personal growth. If it does not evoke a sense of excitement and challenge, it may be too attainable.

4. **Document Your Goal:**
Write down your goal explicitly. Scientific research has shown that writing down a goal can increase your chances of achieving it by up to 42%. This is not a magical trick; it is a simple yet effective strategy that enhances focus and commitment.

5. **Implement a System:**
A bold and aligned goal without a systematic approach is unlikely to be achieved. Consider implementing the following strategies:

- **Writing a Book:** Dedicate 30 minutes each day to writing your book.
- **Public Speaking:** Join a local group or pitch events to develop your public speaking skills.
- **Job Transition:** Start networking, saving, and building a professional bridge to your desired job.

Remember, significant goals do not require extraordinary leaps; they require consistent effort and progress.

Let me clarify: This is not about aspiring to grandiose goals solely for the sake of ego. It is about finally daring to design your life around what truly matters to you.

And that is where confidence becomes unstoppably powerful. Not because everything is flawless or because you are perpetually fearless. But because now, you have consciously chosen boldness.

The version of yourself who already possesses this goal already exists. Your purpose is not to find her; it is to become her—one aligned, audacious, and transformative decision at a time.

Becoming the Person Who Guides Your Life, Not Simply Survives It

Let us acknowledge the truth: Most individuals are merely surviving their lives, not truly living them.

They are not steering the ship; they are merely attempting to prevent it from sinking.

Wake up, scroll through social media, work, people-please, overthink, and crash. Repeat. Days blur into weeks, and before you realise it, you are operating on autopilot, pursuing obligations rather than pursuing dreams, reacting rather than leading.

If this resonates deeply with you, you are not fundamentally flawed. You are merely trapped in survival mode. And survival mode is alluring. It feels familiar, secure. However, here is the unspoken truth:

You were not constructed solely for coping. You were crafted to create.

You were not placed here to live under your potential, to diminish, to settle for "adequate."

You are here to lead. To design. To take control.

And becoming the person who guides your life? That does not entail being assertive or authoritarian. It does not imply becoming an idealised version of a "girlboss" who never wavers in self-assurance.

It is about asserting ownership.

Here's what that looks like:

1. Cease outsourcing your direction.

No one else has the authority to determine what is important to you. Not your friends, not your supervisor, not even your partner. When you lead your life, you cease to anticipate an elusive permission slip.

You do not require someone to "select you." You select yourself.

2. Make decisions, even when they evoke apprehension.

Leaders do not await absolute readiness. They take action, make choices, and trust that they will discern the solution along the way.

Survival mode posits, “What if I fail?” Leadership asserts, “If I remain stagnant, I will deteriorate.”

You lead your life when you accept the job, launch the podcast, establish boundaries, initiate the business—prior to achieving comfort.

3. Cultivate your confidence through challenging endeavours.

Confidence is not bestowed; it is earned. In the small, daunting moments when you choose action over anxiety. Leadership is a muscle. Each time you act in accordance with your future self, you are lifting the weight.

When you rise early to work on your aspiration—leadership. When you finally decline what drains you—leadership. When you speak the truth, even if your voice trembles—leadership.

4. Cease managing others’ opinions and focus on managing your energy.

The more you attempt to control how others perceive you, the more powerless you feel. Individuals will judge you regardless of whether you exhibit smallness or assertiveness—so you may as well pursue what truly matters to you.

Survivors adjust themselves to conform to the prevailing norms. Leaders enter the room and assert their presence.

5. Prioritise self-leadership.

This is a significant undertaking. Leadership is not synonymous with titles or teams. It commences with how you demonstrate self-care. - Do you honour your self-made commitments?- Do you appear when no one is offering accolades?- Do you uphold your values, even when it presents challenges?

That embodies leadership. And when you lead yourself, others become aware. Not because you are more vocal—but because you are more articulate. Regarding your direction, your worth, and your purpose.

Self-Assessment: Are You Surviving or Leading?

Reflect on your life: Are you merely existing or actively guiding your journey?

Becoming the leader of your life does not commence with perfection. It begins with ceasing to wait, apologising, and making deliberate choices—with clarity, courage, and consistency.

No one will rescue you; however, you possess the power to lead yourself.

By embracing this role, transformative change will ensue.

The Final Confrontation: Your Confidence Manifesto

Be candid: Your pursuit of confidence extends beyond mere comprehension; it aims to construct and embody it, liberating yourself from self-imposed limitations.

You have diligently studied the narratives, delved into the scientific principles, and practised the practical tools. Now, it is time to assert and fully embrace your confidence.

This serves as a defining moment.

Confidence is not an ephemeral emotion; it is a conscious decision to live it every day.

Therefore, I present to you a manifesto—a resolute declaration of your identity and your leadership principles for the future.

My Personal Growth and Development Plan

1. Embrace Courage and Confidence:
- Act decisively rather than waiting for readiness.
- Recognise that courage precedes confidence.
- Use fear as a guiding principle, not a limiting factor.
- Embrace fear as a catalyst for action, even when it feels daunting.

2. Take Responsibility and Self-Leadership:
- Reframe the mindset from survival to leadership.
- Cease seeking permission and assert your independence.
- Create your own seat at the table or build a new one if necessary.
- Understand that you are not meant to be picked; you are meant to choose yourself.

3. Embrace Authenticity and Self-Expression:
- Refrain from conforming to societal expectations and embrace your true self.
- Avoid shrinking to fit in and stand up for your individuality.
- Speak up confidently, even when your voice trembles.

- Recognise that silence hinders the expression of your truth.

4. Develop Trust in Yourself and Your Capabilities:
- Trust your inner wisdom and intuition to guide you.
- Recognise that you do not require every answer to take the first step.
- Self-back yourself and follow through with your actions.
- Demonstrate reliability by consistently showing up, especially in challenging situations.

5. Honour Your Commitments and Self-Care:
- Treat yourself with respect and reverence, as you would a valued friend.
- Maintain a sacred relationship with yourself by keeping your promises, even in small matters.
- Learn from your experiences and use them as stepping stones for growth.
- Embrace setbacks as opportunities for learning and improvement.

6. Cultivate Confidence Through Action and Clarity:
- Develop confidence through consistent action and clarity.
- Engage in purposeful activities that align with your goals and values.
- Maintain a positive outlook and maintain a sense of self-assurance.
- Recognise that confidence is not a passive trait; it is a result of taking proactive steps.

7. Live Authentically and Unapologetically:
- Embrace your true self and live authentically.
- Refrain from compromising your values or beliefs.
- Communicate your thoughts and feelings openly and honestly.
- Be confident in your abilities and embrace your uniqueness.

8. Embrace Self-Discovery and Personal Growth:
- Continuously seek self-discovery and personal growth opportunities.
- Explore new experiences and perspectives that enrich your life.
- Develop self-awareness and self-acceptance to foster personal growth.
- Embrace the journey of self-discovery and live life to the fullest.

This is not merely a list; it serves as your guiding principle.

Print it, disseminate it, and immerse yourself in its content until it becomes an automatic process. When that familiar voice emerges, assailing you with apprehension, revisit the list.

For this is your current state: unapologetic, unwavering, and indomitable.

Let us proceed.

Conclusion: Your Loud Life Begins Now

Let us cease to feign the necessity of additional time. More time to contemplate. More time to prepare. More time to feel "ready." This is the most antiquated fallacy in existence, and let us be candid, it has kept you ensnared for an extended period.

For here lies the truth you already possess: you are not awaiting confidence. Confidence is the one who awaits you.

You have successfully completed this book. This achievement is not insignificant. It signifies your determination to transcend your limitations and embrace a more expansive, audacious, and courageous existence.

Now, it is time to take decisive action.

You do not require a complete overhaul of your life tomorrow. This is not about monumental, dramatic transformations—it is about making incremental decisions, one at a time. One micro-act of courage. One courageous conversation. One moment when you silence your inner critic and proceed regardless.

You do not need to be fearless. You merely need to navigate life with fear as a constant presence, but not as the driver of your vehicle.

Furthermore, do not deceive yourself into believing that this journey will be devoid of challenges, elegance, or tranquility. It will be messy. You will make mistakes. You will stumble over your words.

You will doubt yourself and yearn to retreat into the comfort of familiarity.

However, you will not achieve this goal. Now that you possess knowledge and tools, it is time to take action.

The question arises: what will you do next?

Will you raise your hand when your heart races?

Will you cease rehearsing and begin speaking?

Will you cease waiting for someone to select you—and ultimately choose yourself?

You have one life, and it is not meant to be quiet.

You were created to live loudly, to assert your power, to trust your voice, and to build a life that reflects your true self—not the version you believed others desired.

Therefore, let this serve as your wake-up call, your rallying cry, and your final excuse.

Do not merely read this book; live it.

Raise your hand, speak the truth, enter the room, pose the question, initiate the action, take the shot.

You already possess the knowledge of what to do.

Now execute it.

Your vibrant life commences immediately.

Confidence is Not an Inherent Quality—It is a Choice

Let us clarify that confidence is not an ethereal sensation that emerges when all conditions are ideal.

It is not concealed beneath the bed, lost in the depths of your inbox, or waiting for you at the conclusion of a ten-step self-improvement plan.

Confidence is a decision, a choice you make at this very moment.

It is not about feeling fearless; rather, it is about embracing the fear and proceeding forward.

This is where individuals often falter. They misconceive confidence as a hereditary trait, akin to dimples or long eyelashes.

Contrary to this notion, the process operates differently.

Confidence is not a trait inherent in personality; it is a result of action.

Admirable individuals—those who speak up, raise their hands, initiate projects, share videos, wear bold attire, tell the truth, resign from their positions, and write books—do not possess greater bravery than you.

They have cultivated a habit of acting decisively, choosing boldness over comfort, even when their hands tremble, their voice wavers, and their mind questions their actions.

They persist and act regardless.

This resolute decision—the choice to take action—fosters the very confidence you perceive as innate.

Confidence is akin to a muscle, and it is not developed through mere contemplation. It is forged through consistent effort, through demonstrating presence, and through executing repetitive actions.

Each time you make a decision that aligns with courage rather than comfort, you reinforce the belief: "I possess the ability to trust myself."

This fundamental principle underpins confidence.

It is not about possessing all the answers or being the most proficient in a given field.

It is about trusting your inner voice to manifest regardless of your apprehension.

Therefore, I grant you permission to cease waiting for a "feeling" of confidence.

Simply make a decision: Decide that you are an individual who, despite fear, chooses to take action.

Decide that your voice holds significance.

Determine that you have dedicated sufficient time to the pursuit of a sense of readiness.

Then, take decisive action.

Confidence is not an innate trait; rather, it is a conscious choice made through courageous decisions taken one step at a time.

You Possess All Necessary Resources

Allow me to share a revelation that may profoundly alter your self-perception:

You are not lacking any essential components.

A degree, additional time, an online course, permission, or an inexplicable surge of confidence are not missing from your life.

You already possess the necessary resources to take the next step.

I acknowledge that your mind may resist this notion, likely asserting, “Mel, I am not prepared. I require a comprehensive plan, thorough understanding of the process, and more practical experience. I need clarity and… something more.”

Refrain from succumbing to these apprehensions.

These apprehensions are merely manifestations of fear, and your mind’s excuse-making mechanisms are attempting to maintain your current state of stagnation, safety, and silence.

In essence, you require a profound recollection of your identity.

You have overcome each arduous day that you believed would shatter your resolve. You have endured heartbreak, rejection, failure, and fear, yet you persist. You continue to awaken, dream, and yearn for more.

This signifies something profound.

It implies that you possess an inherent courage within your DNA.

It suggests that you possess the requisite skills to tackle challenging endeavours.

It provides evidence that you can endure discomfort and emerge stronger.

However, it is crucial to acknowledge that you will never attain a state of "feeling readiness." This notion is not applicable to significant life events or genuine personal growth.

Therefore, the confidence you seek will not be derived from waiting.

It emanates from taking action.

It stems from the belief that the tools lie within you, not outside.

It encourages you to act on your instincts rather than succumbing to insecurities.

It underscores the realisation that the answers are not external entities; they reside within you, always have, and will continue to do so.

The sole missing element is your decision to believe it.

Allow me to reiterate this unequivocally:

You possess all the necessary attributes.

The voice.

The strength.

The gut instincts.

The courage.

The spark.

These qualities are already inherent within you. You merely need to cease doubting them long enough to allow them to guide your actions.

Now, seize this truth and proceed with the task you have been postponing.

For this is not about transforming into a new individual.

It is about becoming the authentic version of yourself.

The Time for Procrastination Has Expired

Be candid with yourself.

You have been engaged in a state of anticipation.

Anticipating the opportune moment.

Seeking clarity.

Feeling prepared.

Waiting for someone to acknowledge your desire for greater fulfilment.

Waiting for life to stabilise.

Waiting for the apprehension to dissipate.

However, it is imperative that you confront the truth you have been evading: Procrastination is not a form of preparation; it is a disguised manifestation of delay.

The longer you persist in this state of inaction, the more pronounced your doubts become. Your aspirations diminish. The weight of apprehension intensifies within your chest.

Allow me to convey a revelation that may elude others: You do not require additional time. You must make a decisive choice.

That aspiration? That objective? That conversation you continually replay in your mind? It will not suddenly diminish in apprehension tomorrow. You will not awaken next Monday and magically acquire greater courage.

What truly transforms your life?

Your actions, taken immediately.

I am not suggesting a complete overhaul of your life in a single day. Rather, I am referring to the most minute and courageous decision to take action. To speak up, to commence, to cease hiding, to stop shrinking, and to refrain from saying "maybe later" when what you truly intend is "I am apprehensive."

Surprisingly, everyone experiences fear.

The distinction between individuals who lead fulfilling lives and those who feel trapped lies not in talent, luck, or impeccable timing. It resides in movement.

They have ceased waiting, exhausted by their own excuses, and comprehended that life is not a dress rehearsal—it is an ongoing experience.

Therefore, I urge you to heed this wake-up call:

The time for procrastination has concluded.

This is your life, not a trial, a draft version, or something to refine behind the scenes before publishing. You do not require additional qualifications, nor a plan so meticulously crafted that failure is inconceivable. You merely need one decision that asserts, "I have reached my limit."

For nothing undergoes transformation until you take action.

You have dedicated sufficient time to reading, planning, and dreaming.

Now, it is time to move forward.

You are prepared—Even If You Are Afraid

Allow me to dispel the misconception that fear implies a lack of readiness.

Feeling apprehensive does not signify a lack of preparedness.

It signifies your humanity, your compassion, and your imminent engagement in a significant endeavour.

You have been conditioned to believe that "readiness" is an emotional state. That one day, you will awaken, stretch, sip your coffee, and suddenly, confidence will burst through the window, exclaiming, "Let us proceed, my esteemed individual!"

That day? It will not materialise.

For readiness is not an emotion; it is a conscious choice.

In essence, you possess the necessary qualities to achieve your goals, albeit you have yet to demonstrate them effectively.

Let us examine the facts: you possess the knowledge, instincts, drive, and an unwavering idea that persists in your mind. You also possess a voice that refuses to remain silent and a burning desire for growth.

The sole obstacle between you and your next level lies in fear—fear of failure, judgment, and even success (admittedly, it is a valid concern).

Fear, incidentally, serves as a signpost, manifesting when you are on the precipice of growth, venturing into uncharted territories, or embarking on transformative journeys.

Therefore, instead of perceiving fear as a hindrance, consider it a catalyst for progress.

Every bold action you have taken, every decision you have made, every step you have taken despite apprehension, has been accompanied by fear.

Despite this, you have persevered and achieved your objectives.

The hallmark of readiness is your presence here, engaged in this reading, yearning for more, and contemplating your future rather than succumbing to the comfort of the past.

Readiness is not absolute certainty; it is a willingness to embrace uncertainty.

It is not the absence of absolute confidence; it is acknowledging your apprehension while choosing to proceed.

Therefore, do not anticipate the complete eradication of fear; it will not occur.

However, your courage flourishes with each action taken amidst apprehension.

The internal voice may persistently whisper doubts, but you need not confront it. Simply take action.

You are ready, even if you experience trepidation.

Now, it is your turn to demonstrate your readiness.

Before You Close This Book...

Take a moment to pause and reflect. Who were you when you first opened these pages? What were the fears, doubts, or habits that held your voice back? Now look at yourself with honest eyes—stronger, clearer, bolder. You have traversed truths and tools that were always yours to claim. So, write it down: who you were before this book and who you are now. Let that transformation reside on paper. For this version of you deserves to be heard—loudly.

About the Author

Rashid Khan, born into a modest family with limited resources, recognised from a young age that life would not provide him with opportunities; he would have to forge them himself. Despite facing numerous challenges, he successfully navigated from scarcity to significance, ascending to become a respected leader and coach at one of the world's leading technology companies. His journey serves as a testament to the transformative power of resilience, determination, and unwavering self-assurance.

However, Rashid's aspirations extended beyond personal success. Over the years, he has dedicated himself to uplifting others. Through mentorship and coaching, he has transformed lives, assisting individuals in rewriting their narratives, rediscovering their inherent value, and finding their rightful place within society. His practical wisdom, authentic communication style, and profound empathy have made him a catalyst for positive change in both professional and personal spheres.

Made in United States
Cleveland, OH
06 July 2025

18295730R00134